A TASTE OF LIVING IN Charleston

LOWCOUNTRY DISHES ANYONE CAN COOK

BOBBY SHEALY

Eleventh-Generation Charlestonian and
National Award-Winning Real Estate Agent

www.mascotbooks.com

A Taste of Living in Charleston: Lowcountry Dishes Anyone Can Cook

Photography by Pam Middleton Hennet.

For more information, please contact:
Mascot Books
620 Herndon Parkway, Suite 320
Herndon, VA 20170
info@mascotbooks.com

Library of Congress Control Number: 2021909908

CPSIA Code: PRQ0521A
ISBN-13: 978-1-64543-493-1

Printed in India

This book is dedicated to two angels:

My mother above, Marjorie Roddey Shealy (Snookie), who taught me to entertain by example, and my angel on earth, my dear friend, Jennifer Finger Krause, whose constant support, enthusiasm, and drive are the force behind me. Without her, this book would have never become a reality.

INTRODUCTION

*T*he idea for this book was suggested by friends at a supper party one night because they enjoyed my food so much. My reply was always, "If I can cook it, so can you!" People love delicious Southern food, and they are totally capable of making it, but they claim they just don't have time to cook. This book provides many shortcuts to fabulous (mostly Southern) recipes. If you are afraid of fat and gravies and bacon and butter and cheese and sour cream . . . this isn't the book for you. I am the cook, not the doctor!

I must confess, there are a couple of recipes I could not shorten. They are just too delicious in their traditional format, and there was no way to change them without sacrificing their unbelievable, rich flavors. One of which is the *real* homemade banana pudding (page 150)!

The recipes in this book are an accumulation of more than forty years of cooking. I collected some from family and friends. I created some, and I re-purposed others to create my own twists. A few were originals that had to be repeated and passed down because they were too good not to share.

I hope these recipes bring as much happiness to my readers' tables as they have mine. There have been a lot of love, good times, friendships, and relationships cultivated over my food. My wish is that these become traditions for others, as well.

I grew up in a typical Southern family where we gathered every Sunday and every holiday over lots of delicious food. On Sundays, my Moma (the world spells it "Momma," but this is how we spelled it) and Moms (my dad's mother) would rotate who hosted and who fixed the main course, dessert, and side dishes. (We need to get something clear, as well, about Southern traditions: Dinner is lunch, and supper is dinner. So, when you are asked to Sunday dinner, that means the meal at lunchtime after church.)

All my life, food was a big thing in our house. My dad was an avid hunter and fisherman, so fresh game and fish were always in the freezer. Dada (my dad's father) tended to a very large vegetable garden. I was taught even before I started first grade how to check the watermelons and cantaloupes to see if they were ready for picking and what size squash and okra should be before picking. We also learned when to grab the tomatoes off the bush before the birds figured out they were almost ripe and how to husk corn while still on the stalk to check if it was ready. I remember a time when I was about five years old, sitting on the porch at my family's house on Sullivan's Island. I was picking blue crab that Daddy must have caught. Later, we lived on the water and caught shrimp like you have never seen. We baited (when there were no laws to the contrary) with laying pellets (chicken food), and it was normal to catch twenty-five or more pounds each night off the dock right there in front of the house on Wadmalaw Sound in Meggett, South Carolina, twenty-five miles south of Charleston. Fresh meat, seafood, and vegetables were the staples of my life.

I come from a long line of good cooks. I remember my great-grandmother, Naomi Bailey Welch (we called her Mama), always had a pot of something smelling glorious on her stove every time I walked in the door. Moms (Mama's daughter and my grandmother) cooked wonderful roasts and vegetables and red rice and cakes and fried chicken and shrimp—the list goes on. Then, there was my Moma. People called her Snookie. She was a glamorous and beautiful lady, a fabulous cook, and she and Daddy entertained quite often. Moma always catered her own parties and dinners, no matter how large the guest list. I remember before parties, she would be making cheese balls and rolling meatballs, and our housekeeper, Elizabeth, would be peeling pounds of shrimp.

Today, I laugh when I hear parents say their child won't eat this or that. We would *never* have said we weren't going to eat something. It just wasn't allowed. But then, the issue never came up!

We lived on Sullivan's Island in the 1960s and early '70s. Growing up, my older sister, Debbie, and I were trained on how to mix cocktails for my parents' friends who dropped by. So, if Mr. Jones dropped in, we would ask him what he would like to drink. If he replied a bourbon and Coke, then I got the excitement of loading up the glass with ice, Debbie poured the bourbon, and I topped it off with the Coke.

This started when we were about ten and thirteen years old, and it continued until we graduated from high school. The rule was to fill the glass to the top with ice, make everyone's first drink a double, and top it off with the mixer. When they got a little buzz, we would switch them to the cheap liquor! This rule was strictly adhered to when we (and our friends) bartended for my parents' parties. Daddy often reiterated that everyone's first drink be a double. We thought it was great fun! Those were the times then, and it was perfectly acceptable.

Charleston is quite the cocktail town. There are cocktails for everything at every hour. That's how it has always been as long as I can remember. The big joke is, "How many Charlestonians does it take to change a light bulb? It takes three: One to hold the ladder, one to change the light bulb, and one to mix the cocktails!"

Someone visiting once asked me, "What time is cocktail hour?" My reply was, "As soon as you open the bottle 'cause it's five o'clock somewhere!" You do know that you can't drink all day unless you start in the morning! Another note on Southern tradition: Cocktail hour is actually an hour and fifteen minutes. That's my rule, and I'm stretching it a little. Supper is served within an hour and thirty minutes from the appointed time of arrival.

Growing up around great food, entertaining parties, and fun people, how could I not have a love of it all? The greatest compliment, I believe, is for someone to invite you to their home—whether it be for cocktails or dinner or a party.

I love to feed people. I love the feeling I get seeing people take pleasure in what I have cooked and planned. It's a win-win. They get pleasure from eating, and I get pleasure watching them eat what I have created. The power of food is far-reaching. It brings people together around a table, bonding and connecting. It is used to celebrate happy times, like weddings and birthdays, and it's there to provide comfort in sad times.

Meals create an intimate time with family and friends, no matter if it's for two people or twelve people. I love to decorate the table with twinkling lights, candles, and flowers—all of which can be done on any budget. Add everything together and dim the lights, and you have an elegant table and soothing ambience.

The purpose of this book is to show any cook, experienced or not, that you can prepare delicious, gorgeous meals with shortcuts. You can make several dishes in advance and freeze them, so there is minimal effort on the day you are entertaining. You can have your appetizer and dessert made and waiting in the freezer, and you can make entrées and side dishes the day before. This way, on the day of your party, your tasks are few, making it easy to put it all together and focus on enjoying time with your loved ones.

Life is busy, and this book makes it easy to cook and enjoy good food without the stress and time commitment. If I can cook it, so can you.

ABOUT THE AUTHOR

A descendant of Captain Robert Seabrook—who arrived in Charleston in 1680—Bobby Shealy is an eleventh-generation Charlestonian and member of The Society of First Families of South Carolina 1670 to 1700, where he served a two-year term as Chairman of the Hospitality and Entertainment Committee. Born and raised in Charleston, South Carolina, Bobby is a retired Administrative Hearing Officer for the South Carolina state government.

Bobby has been a real estate agent in Charleston since 2000 and is a long-standing member of the Charleston Top Producers Club. He has been awarded numerous real estate awards over the years, including Realtor of Distinction and Best Realtor in Charleston. He is the winner of the 2018 and 2019 ERA Franchise Sapphire Award (the highest distinction in luxury real estate for ERA Realty in the nation). He was also named a Top Residential Sales Agent in South Carolina for 2019 and has made appearances on HGTV's *House Hunters*.

In his free time, Bobby is an avid cook and gardener. His garden has been featured in *Southern Living*® magazine, and he is a member of the International Association of Culinary Professionals (IACP). He is also very active in St. Stephen's Episcopal Church, which was the first free church in America, and volunteers for the Berkeley County Guardian Ad Litem Program.

This cookbook blends two of Bobby's biggest passions—real estate and cooking. Please feel free to call on Bobby for all of your real estate needs in Charleston.

PROCEEDS BENEFIT

Pet Helpers
Adoption Center
Spay/Neuter Clinic

Pet Helpers Adoption Center and Spay/Neuter Clinic
is a 501(c)3 non-profit animal welfare organization
dedicated to saving the lives of adoptable animals.
Since its founding in 1978, Pet Helpers has saved
more than 50,000 lives through the generous
support of the Charleston community.

For more information, visit
PETHELPERS.ORG

ACKNOWLEDGMENTS

I must give a huge thank you and credit to my close friend, Pam Middleton Hennet, whose creativity brought this book to life in so many ways with her gorgeous and stunning photography. She is a very talented lady in so many ways. Her contributions were countless and tremendous! Another big thank you to my dear friend, Melissa Van Camp, for her assistance with editing.

A big thank you to Chad and Julia Drayton for the location shoot for the cover and loaning us an original chair from Drayton Hall Estate, which dates back to the 1740s. The chair was the chamber pot used well over two hundred years ago by the Drayton descendants.

A big thank you to Nathalie Dupree, whose graciousness is never ending and was the catalyst that got me pointed in the right direction to start the book.

Thank you to Cynthia Stevens Graubart and Virginia Willis for tremendous guidance from the first day I sat in on one of their courses on how to write a cookbook, which was suggested by Nathalie Dupree.

To Hanna Raskin, Susan Pollak, Brett Mckee, and Eddie Wilder, along with Nathalie Dupree—who provided heartwarming reviews—I can never thank you enough for your support.

Last but not least, a huge thank you to my editor, Nicole Hall. Her professionalism, guidance, and patience with me made the journey extremely enjoyable.

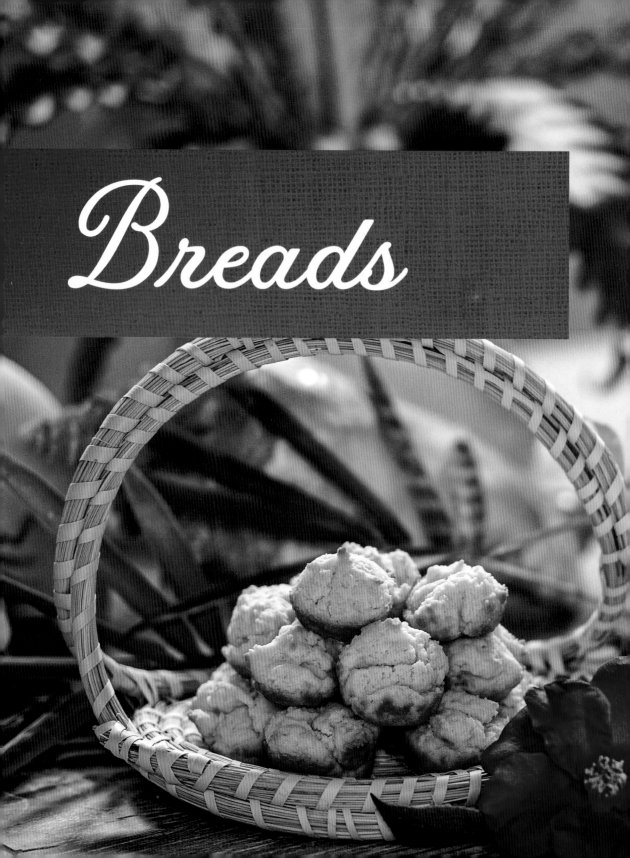

Breads

MOMS' BEER LOAF

SERVING SIZE: 6 | **PREP TIME:** 10 MINS | **COOKING TIME:** 1 HOUR

I found this in my grandmother, Frances Welch Shealy's (Moms), recipes on a piece of scratch paper in her handwriting. It makes the most delicious, gorgeous loaf of bread. It can also be frozen and brought out later. Throw some butter on it and enjoy.

INGREDIENTS

- 3 cups self-rising flour
- 1 12-ounce bottle beer of choice (I used a Pale Ale)
- 3 tablespoons sugar

NOTE: I find that different types of beer change the flavor, so if you're a beer lover, you'll have an edge on the rest of us. When Moms made this, I doubt they had but a few different types of beer available. For a treat, slice the bread, cover in butter, and bake in oven at 350 until edges turn light brown. Makes a fabulous toast as a side for any meal.

DIRECTIONS

1. Preheat oven to 300 degrees Fahrenheit.

2. In a large bowl, mix all ingredients by hand.

3. Pour batter into a greased 9.25 x 5.25-inch loaf pan.

4. Bake for one hour.

MOMA'S SOUR CREAM BISCUITS

| **SERVING SIZE:** 25 | **PREP TIME:** 10 MINS | **COOKING TIME:** 12 MINS |

*M*oma made these all the time. Yummy is the best word to describe them.

INGREDIENTS

- 2 cups Bisquick
- 1 stick (8 tablespoons) butter, softened
- 1 8-ounce container sour cream

NOTE: The great thing about these is they can be made in advance and frozen! Pull them out as needed, let them thaw, and put them in the oven for a few minutes at 350 to warm up.

DIRECTIONS

1. Preheat oven to 400 degrees Fahrenheit.

2. Put Bisquick in a medium bowl and stir with a fork or spoon to get all the lumps out.

3. Cream butter and sour cream in separate bowl.

4. Add Bisquick to wet ingredients, mixing well.

5. Spoon batter into greased, small muffin tins.

6. Cook up to 12 minutes. Watch closely so they do not burn.

Breakfast & Brunch

BAKED BREAKFAST BISCUITS

| **SERVING SIZE:** 8 | **PREP TIME:** 20 MINS | **COOKING TIME:** 10 TO 15 MINS |

This is an easy and delicious take on creating your own breakfast puff pastry. I think of it as a great way to turn left-overs into breakfast. Get creative! Experiment with leftover turkey, dressing, and gravy. Perhaps shrimp and grits? Or turn it into a mini crab puff pastry. Lots of possibilities with this one! Also, if you're having company, you can cook the sausage, bell pepper, and onions the day before to make it easier on yourself.

INGREDIENTS

- 1 large package buttermilk biscuits (6 to 8 in a pack)
- 1 pound hot sausage such as Jimmy Dean
- 1 green bell pepper, chopped
- 1 medium sweet or Vidalia onion, chopped
- 1 16-ounce container sour cream
- 1 8-ounce bag of your favorite cheese (shredded)

DIRECTIONS

1. Preheat oven to 350 degrees Fahrenheit.

2. Remove biscuits from package and separate on a cutting board. Flatten each one, being careful not to tear them. Coat a nonstick muffin pan with cooking spray.

3. Brown sausage in a skillet. Transfer browned sausage to a paper towel-lined plate and set aside. Sauté bell pepper and onion in sausage drippings. Line each muffin tin with the flattened-out biscuit. In each biscuit-lined muffin cup, put a large spoonful of sausage, followed by a spoonful of the onion and bell pepper mixture. Top this with a generous amount of sour cream and then with cheese. Take the four corners of the biscuit and pull up to twist together above the filling. Use your fingers to seal each biscuit. Make sure all creases are sealed.

4. Bake until biscuits are light brown. Remove from tins after cooling a few minutes. Serve warm.

BRIE SAUSAGE BRUNCH CASSEROLE

SERVING SIZE: 6 | **PREP TIME:** 15 MINS | **COOKING TIME:** 50 MINS

*C*razy story on this one—I was at a weekend house party and made this for breakfast. The next morning, we pulled the leftovers out, someone dipped a cracker into it and ate it, and holy moly, we found it to be delicious as a dip! You should warm it back up a little, though. A great brunch menu would be adding a Caesar Salad with smoked oysters, baked pineapple casserole, and Bloody Marys and Mimosas.

INGREDIENTS

- 1 8-ounce round brie
- 1 pound hot pork sausage
- 6 slices white bread (without crust)
- 1 cup grated parmesan cheese
- 7 large eggs
- 3 cups whipping cream, divided
- 2 cups fat-free milk
- 1 tablespoon chopped fresh (or 1 teaspoon dried) rubbed sage
- 1 teaspoon seasoned salt
- 1 teaspoon dry mustard
- 1 small bag slivered almonds

DIRECTIONS

1. Preheat oven to 350 degrees Fahrenheit.

2. Trim and discard rind from top and sides of brie. Cut cheese into cubes and set aside.

3. Cook sausage in a large skillet over medium-high heat, stirring until crumbled and no longer pink; drain well.

4. Lay the bread on the bottom of a lightly greased 13 x 9-inch baking dish. Layer evenly with sausage, brie, and Parmesan cheese.

5. In a large bowl, whisk together 5 eggs, 2 cups whipping cream, milk, sage, salt, and mustard. Pour evenly over cheese and sausage. Cover and chill for 8 hours.

6. Whisk together remaining 2 eggs and 1 cup whipping cream. Pour evenly over chilled mixture.

7. Bake for 50 minutes or until set. Sprinkle with slivered almonds if desired.

MOMA'S BREAKFAST SHRIMP

| **SERVING SIZE:** 4 TO 6 | **PREP TIME:** 15 MINS | **COOKING TIME:** 50 MINS |

*Y*ou can't ever have too many shrimp recipes when you live in Charleston, especially if you live on the river and can catch them regularly. This is a great dish to serve for breakfast with sausages on the side and maybe a biscuit or two! Pairs well with a Dreamsicle Mimosa (page 25).

INGREDIENTS

- 6 slices of bacon
- 1 medium onion, chopped
- ½ green pepper, chopped
- 2 tablespoons all-purpose flour
- 1 pound uncooked shrimp, peeled and tails removed
- Dash or two Tabasco
- Dash salt
- 1 teaspoon Worcestershire sauce
- 4 to 6 tablespoons tomato ketchup
- ½ cup heavy cream

DIRECTIONS

1. Fry bacon in a large frying pan until crisp. Remove bacon and set aside.

2. Sauté onion and bell pepper in bacon grease until tender. Stir in flour, sprinkling a little at a time, and mix well.

3. Turn up heat and add shrimp. They will turn pink when done, but check to make sure they are cooked through. Shrimp don't take but a few minutes to cook.

4. Add enough water to cover shrimp and stir until mixture thickens.

5. Add Tabasco, salt, Worcestershire sauce, and ketchup. Simmer on low heat about 5 minutes.

6. Crumble cooked bacon on top. I'm a taster, so add more of any of the seasonings to taste.

7. Last, but not least, mix in cream and stir well. Serve immediately over grits.

NOTE: Moma cooked this dish all the time but never for breakfast—always for dinner and sometimes for supper. She had gotten the recipe from our close family friend, Emily Whaley, and Emily had said that she got it from her mother-in-law. We lived on the river where fresh shrimp were the norm.

As for the grits, who has time to cook grits for an extended period? Quick grits is the way to go. I use cream instead of water to beef them up, and of course drop a stick of butter in them, as well. Make your grits first and have them ready. The breakfast shrimp cooks pretty quick.

CRAB QUICHE

SERVING SIZE: 6 | **PREP TIME:** 10 MINS | **COOKING TIME:** 30 TO 40 MINS

My good friend, Debbie Jordan, gave me this recipe years ago. She is such a great cook, and we have traded recipes for over 30 years.

INGREDIENTS

- ½ cup mayonnaise
- 2 tablespoons all-purpose flour
- 2 beaten eggs
- ½ cup milk
- 1 7.5-ounce can crab meat
- 8 ounces Swiss cheese, grated
- Sliced green onions
- 1 9-inch deep-dish pie shell

NOTE: You can play with this recipe and add or subtract more cheese to your liking, or experiment with your favorite cheese rather than using Swiss cheese. Lump crab meat or fresh crab is great. Add a little extra to your liking. This is really good paired with my Baked Pineapple. One more thing! A Bloody Mary, screwdriver, or mimosa will top it off!

DIRECTIONS

1. Preheat oven to 350 degrees Fahrenheit.

2. Mix the first four ingredients together in a bowl.

3. Add remaining ingredients, mix well, and pour into unbaked pie shell.

4. Bake for 40 to 45 minutes.

BAKED PINEAPPLE

This is my standard sweet dish for a brunch. It goes well with crab quiche and a Caesar salad. (You can buy a delicious Caesar salad kit these days, so don't bother making it from scratch.) I like to add smoked oysters to the Caesar salad in place of the anchovies. The flavors blend incredibly well, and it's all so delicious. A mimosa is the perfect addition.

INGREDIENTS

- 1 20-ounce can pineapple chunks, drained
- 1 cup grated sharp cheddar cheese
- ⅓ cup sugar
- 3 tablespoons self-rising flour
- 1 stick (8 tablespoons) butter, melted
- 1 (full size) roll Ritz crackers

DIRECTIONS

1. Preheat oven to 325 degrees Fahrenheit.

2. Drain pineapple and pour into an 8 x 8-inch baking dish.

3. Combine cheese, sugar, and flour in a separate bowl and pour over pineapple.

4. Melt butter in a dish large enough to hold the crackers. Mash the crackers to soak in melted butter.

5. Pour crackers and butter over pineapple mixture.

6. Bake for 20 to 25 minutes.

THE BEST MOIST SAUSAGE BALLS

SERVING SIZE: 30 BALLS | **PREP TIME:** 15 MINS | **COOKING TIME:** 20-25 MINS

When I think of sausage balls, my mind always goes back to the ones that everyone always brought to some event. I knew, no matter what, they were going to be dry, and I was going to eat them anyway and make the best out of it rather than go hungry. But these are different—very moist and yummy. Can't eat just one! Or two, for that matter! These can be made and frozen uncooked. Pull them out of the freezer and cook them as you need them. A great treat, yet again, from cooking talk with my good friend, Debbie Jordan.

INGREDIENTS

- 8 ounces cream cheese, softened
- 1 pound hot sausage
- 1 ¼ cup Bisquick
- 4 ounces sharp cheddar cheese, grated

DIRECTIONS

1. Preheat oven to 400 degrees Fahrenheit.

2. Mix all ingredients thoroughly. The best way might be with an electric mixer, but I usually squeeze the dough between my fingers.

3. Roll into 1-inch balls and place on tin foil-lined cookie sheet.

4. Bake for about 20 to 25 minutes or until brown.

TOMATO GRITS CASSEROLE

SERVING SIZE: 6 | **PREP TIME:** 15 MINS | **COOKING TIME:** 30 MINS

*C*an't get any more Southern than tomatoes and grits. This is so easy, and I serve it every year at my tree trimming party. Always devoured! Thank you again, Karen Paciulan.

INGREDIENTS

- 8 slices bacon
- 2 cups chicken broth
- Dash salt
- 1 cup quick grits
- 1 16-ounce can diced tomatoes
- 1 cup cheddar cheese, grated

NOTE: I add ground sausage or shrimp to make this a main dish.

DIRECTIONS

1. Cook bacon until crisp in a medium to large pot.

2. Slowly add broth, then add a dash of salt and bring to a boil.

3. Stir in grits and tomatoes and return to a boil, stirring often.

4. Reduce heat and simmer for about 15 to 20 minutes, stirring often.

5. Stir in cheese. Cover and let stand 5 minutes.

Cocktails

REAL EGGNOG

SERVING SIZE: 15   **PREP TIME:** 25 MINS

*I*f you have not figured it out yet, cocktails are a way of life in Charleston, and boy, oh boy, oh boy—this is the real Mc-Coy! My good friend, Taylor Boyd, gave me this recipe. It came from an old handwritten recipe that had been passed down in his family. The only thing I changed was increasing the amount of rum! I serve this every year at my tree trimming party, and it's a hit, to say the least. It is very luscious as the cream turns to a yummy, thick foam and rises to the top. Beware—it's very potent.

INGREDIENTS

- 1 dozen eggs
- 1 ½ cups sugar, divided
- 1 quart milk
- 1 quart whipping cream
- 1 quart bourbon whiskey
- ¼ quart light rum (optional)

DIRECTIONS

1. Separate your egg whites and yolks, reserving both in separate dishes. (You can get a sweet little contraption that does this for you.)

2. Add 1 cup sugar to the yolks and beat well with an electric mixer.

3. Slowly add ½ cup sugar to the whites while beating with the mixer.

4. Combine yolks and whites into large bowl. Stir in milk and cream and add the booze! Stir gently to combine.

5. Refrigerate to chill before serving. Should be made 1 day in advance.

VODKA PUNCH

SERVING SIZE: 15 TO 20 | **PREP TIME:** 10 MINS

I got this in the late '80s from a friend named Andy Werts who said it was his family's party punch recipe. I have made it countless times over the years. My church group especially loves it, but then again, we are Episcopalians! When my niece, Lindsay, got married, we used it as a signature cocktail in a large champagne fountain, and it was quite glorious. This is wonderful for a large gathering. I served it on a hot day for a pool party. Seemed like a good idea at the time. Uber got a lot of business that night.

INGREDIENTS

- 1 2-quart bottle of Cranberry Juice Cocktail
- 1 2-quart bottle of unsweetened pineapple juice
- 1 2-quart bottle of ginger ale
- 1 1.75-liter bottle of vodka (buy an extra bottle to add more if desired)

DIRECTIONS

1. Chill all ingredients. Combine all into a punch bowl, and you are set to go.

NOTE: I have an old punch bowl mold that my Great-Aunt Lucy used to freeze pineapple chunks, cherries, and ginger ale in. I place this in the middle of the punch bowl for a little extra show.

THE EXECUTIVE MARTINI

SERVING SIZE: 2   **PREP TIME:** 15 MINS

*C*harleston being the cocktail town it is, you must have your go-to drink. Then your second go-to drink. This is my first go-to: a vodka martini, dirty, straight up, with blue cheese-stuffed olives. Yeah, baby! My second is a Manhattan on the rocks, not straight up. This recipe makes two martinis. Three would put me under the table.

INGREDIENTS

- 1 ounce dry vermouth
- 1 cup ice cubes
- 6 ounces preferred vodka
- 6 blue cheese-stuffed olives
- Olive juice

DIRECTIONS

1. Chill 2 martini glasses.

2. Pour vermouth into a martini shaker. Swish it around and then toss it out.

3. Add ice cubes and vodka; let chill, usually about 5 to 8 minutes.

4. Put 3 blue cheese-stuffed olives on a toothpick.

5. Pour vodka into martini glasses, then add olive juice to taste to "dirty" it up, depending on how dirty you like it.

6. Add olives, then relax and enjoy. If it's just you, there's another martini in the shaker for you.

TEQUILA AVOCADOS

SERVING SIZE: 4 | **PREP TIME:** 15 MINS

*Y*es, yes, yes! My friends, Rhett Thurmond and Harry Clark, are the ultimate hosts and created this fun and tasty appetizer. They serve them in wonderful little square dishes with a spoon. Their guests sit around the living room enjoying these tasty treats with the tequila bottle sitting on the coffee table for additional splashes. Everyone who tries this loves it!

INGREDIENTS

- 2 ripe avocados
- Juice of 2 limes
- Margarita salt
- Tequila

DIRECTIONS

1. Cut avocados in half and remove pit.

2. Brush each half with lime juice and sprinkle with salt.

3. Set avocado halves in a small bowl or container, and fill holes with tequila.

4. Eat with a spoon. Keep tequila and salt handy to add more as you eat.

DREAMSICLE MIMOSA

SERVING SIZE: 4   **PREP TIME:** 15 MINS

The original mimosa was named after the yellow flowered mimosa plant in Spain but is also believed to have been invented in 1900 in a hotel in the Mediterranean. The name of this one tells the tale! Talk about delicious! On those hot summer days when you crave creamsicle ice cream, look no further! Talk about the perfect touch to a morning brunch. It's just like eating ice cream with the added benefit of Champagne!

INGREDIENTS

- 1 bottle of your favorite Champagne, ice cold
- 1 52-ounce bottle orange juice
- ¼ cup sugar
- 1 quart heavy cream, ice cold

DIRECTIONS

1. Drop a teaspoon or 2 of sugar in the bottom of a Champagne flute.

2. Fill approximately halfway with Champagne and add orange juice to taste. Fill the rest of the glass with cream.

3. Gently stir, and get ready for takeoff!

NOTE: Prior to serving, I like to put the Champagne, orange juice, and cream in the freezer for about 20 minutes to get them all icy cold!

Appetizers

WICKED CHARLESTON PARTY SAUCE

SERVING SIZE: 10 | **PREP TIME:** 10 MINS

This sauce is going to surprise the heck out of anyone who makes it! My friend, Karen Paciulan, a fabulous cook known for her Christmas Day brunches, told me about it. It is so absolutely delicious and so different. I cover a softened block of cream cheese with it and serve it with Ritz crackers. Can't get any easier, and I promise it's a huge winner and no effort. I like to keep a container of this sauce in the refrigerator over the Christmas holidays along with a block of cream cheese. That way, I have an appetizer ready at a moment's notice.

INGREDIENTS

- 1 18-ounce jar apple jelly
- 1 18-ounce jar pineapple preserves
- 1 ounce dry mustard
- 1 5-ounce jar prepared horseradish

DIRECTIONS

1. Combine all ingredients until well blended. Serve over cream cheese.

2. Sauce will keep in the refrigerator in a covered bowl for about 2 weeks.

NOTE: Believe it or not, pineapple preserves can be hard to locate. I have found them at Walmart and on Amazon.

DELICIOUS LIVER PÂTÉ

SERVING SIZE: 2 SMALL TINS | **PREP TIME:** 30 MINS | **COOKING TIME:** 20 MINS

*M*y research tells me that pâté originated in Belgium and is always made with some sort of liver.

This version is always a hit, even with those folks who claim they don't like liver!

INGREDIENTS

- 1 medium onion, chopped
- Olive oil for sautéing
- 1 pound chicken livers
- 1 pound hot bulk sausage (I like Jimmy Dean.)
- ½ teaspoon salt
- 1 teaspoon ground oregano
- 1 teaspoon ground thyme
- ⅛ teaspoon cayenne pepper
- ⅛ teaspoon ground nutmeg
- 3 tablespoons dried parsley

DIRECTIONS

1. Sauté onion in oil until tender, using enough oil to sauté but not cover the onion.

2. Add chicken livers and cook until light pink in color.

3. Mix in sausage; cook 15 minutes or until sausage appears to be done. If the mixture looks excessively wet or is sitting in oil, drain a little.

4. Add seasonings and mix well.

5. Remove from heat and grind in a food processor for 2 minutes. Pack mixture into two 1-pound mini loaf pans.

6. Cover and refrigerate until firm. Serve with crackers.

NOTE: This recipe is great because it makes two tins. You can serve one and freeze the other for a future event. It will freeze well for at least three months.

AUNT LUCY'S CHEESE BISCUITS & RHETT THURMAN'S CHEESE CRACKERS

SERVING SIZE: 25 | **PREP TIME:** 20 MINS | **COOKING TIME:** 12 TO 15 MINS

*C*heese cookies, cheese biscuits, cheese straws, cheese wafers. Cheese thingies are a way of Southern life. At parties, during the holidays, with a cocktail in the afternoon, or just for a treat; cheese cookies have been around forever. This is my Aunt Lucy's recipe, but after a little research, I found the same recipe—or a version thereof—in cookbook after cookbook, so who knows who can actually claim it. The great thing about both Lucy's and Rhett's recipes is you can freeze them! You can bring them out as you need them—just take out a handful, thaw, and treat yourself to a cheese biscuit along with your favorite cocktail, of course! I have baked them on cookie sheets, and I have mashed them down in tiny muffin tins to make little thin coins. My friend, Mary Greene, makes the best I have ever had, and sadly, I've never been able to match hers. They are light and fluffy; obviously she's using a technique passed down to her. Seems everyone's texture is a little different, but the flavor is always delicious. You can't eat just one!

INGREDIENTS

LUCY'S:

- ½ pound sharp cheddar cheese, grated
- ½ pound butter or 8 ounces Oleo, softened
- ½ teaspoon salt
- ¼ teaspoon red pepper
- 2 cups all-purpose flour
- 2 cups Rice Krispies

RHETT'S:

- ½ pound butter, softened
- ½ pound sharp cheddar cheese, grated
- 2 cups all-purpose flour
- ¼ to ½ teaspoon salt
- ¼ teaspoon red pepper
- Usually about 25 pecan halves

DIRECTIONS

LUCY'S BISCUITS:

1. Preheat oven to 350 degrees Fahrenheit.

2. Cream cheese and butter, mixing well with a hand mixer. Mix salt, red pepper, and flour in a separate bowl. Add flour mixture to cheese and butter and mix well. Add Rice Krispies, mixing well.

3. Drop by the teaspoon onto an ungreased cookie sheet. Bake for 15 minutes. Do not overcook.

RHETT'S CRACKERS:

1. Preheat oven to 425 degrees Fahrenheit.

2. Cream butter and cheese. Add flour, salt, and red pepper. Mix very well and roll into a log. Refrigerate at least an hour.

3. Slice log into ¼-inch coins. Top each coin with a pecan half and bake until coins start to turn brown around the edges, about 10 minutes. Do not overcook.

NOTE: Rhett Thurman and I attend St. Stephen's Episcopal church together. She is a fabulous cook and more so, a very well-known Charleston artist who has achieved national acclaim for both oils and watercolors and for her distinctive style. She and her husband, Harry Clark, are fabulous hosts, and a good time is always had by all at their Charleston home.

BAKED BRIE

SERVING SIZE: 6 | **PREP TIME:** 15 MINS | **COOKING TIME:** 25 MINS

I was in a supper club for ten years. There were six of us, and we ate and drank and cooked our way through our thirties! It was great fun sitting around the table, course after course, each scrumptious, with everyone going above and beyond each time! My good friend, Anne Bagnal, one of the supper club six, shared this particular recipe with me, and it is too easy not to share here. Quick to prepare and absolutely delicious—this is a hit every time I serve it. Once the brie has been eaten, you can break up the leftover bread and eat it, too.

INGREDIENTS

- 1 13.2-ounce brie round
- 1 large round bread
- 1 12-ounce jar seedless raspberry jam
- ½ cup brown sugar
- 1 2.25-ounce bag of almond slices or ½ to ¾ cup chopped walnuts

DIRECTIONS

1. Preheat oven to 350 degrees Fahrenheit.

2. Scrape coating off brie with a knife just like you would a burnt piece of toast.

3. Cut a circle in the top of the bread the size of the brie and deep enough for the brie round to sit even or flush with the top of the bread. Remove cut bread from the circle. You may have to hollow it out with your fingers.

4. Set brie in the hollow and cover thickly with jam. Cover jam with brown sugar, spreading jam and sugar around and down the edges of the cheese. Sprinkle jam and cheese with nuts.

5. Bake for 20 to 30 minutes or until bubbly. Stir and serve warm with crackers or ginger snaps.

SMOKED OYSTER CURRY CHEESE BALL

SERVING SIZE: 1 CHEESEBALL | **PREP TIME:** 15 MINS

*H*ave to give credit where credit is due. I found this in *Charleston Receipts Repeats*, first printing, 1986. I use this recipe all the time. Everyone loves it, and it goes fast. It will also last at least 2 months in the freezer, which makes it a go-to for me!

INGREDIENTS

- 8 ounces cream cheese, softened
- 1 3.66-ounce can smoked oysters, slightly drained
- 1 tablespoon Worcestershire sauce
- ½ teaspoon garlic powder
- 1 teaspoon curry powder
- ¾ cup chopped pecans

DIRECTIONS

1. Combine cream cheese and oysters. Mash oysters well into the cream cheese.

2. Add Worcestershire sauce, garlic powder, and curry powder. Mix well.

3. Form entire mixture into a ball and cover in nuts.

NOTE: I usually form mine on a small, plastic cocktail plate and then wrap it with plastic food wrap using toothpicks to keep it off the ball. Freeze and pull it out the day before serving. While frozen, move to a serving plate and keep refrigerated.

CHICKEN CURRY CREAM CHEESE BALL

SERVING SIZE: 1 CHEESEBALL | **PREP TIME:** 20 MINS

*E*veryone loves this dish! I am always asked for the recipe whenever I serve it.

INGREDIENTS

- 1 8-ounce package cream cheese, softened
- 1 cup cooked chicken, chopped
- ¾ cup almond slivers
- ⅓ cup mayonnaise
- 1 tablespoon curry powder
- ¼ teaspoon salt
- 1 9-ounce jar mango chutney

DIRECTIONS

1. Combine first six ingredients in a medium-size bowl and mix well. Using your hands, form a ball and refrigerate overnight. I usually put it on a small plastic plate and insert toothpicks into the top and cover in Saran wrap.

2. When serving, cover the ball generously in mango chutney. This goes well with Ritz crackers.

NOTE: I buy a baked chicken at the grocery store, pull the meat off the bones, and freeze it. When I need chicken for a recipe, I have it on hand.

FRIED GREEN TOMATOES

| SERVING SIZE: 6 TO 8 | PREP TIME: 10 MINS | COOKING TIME: 6 MINS |

INGREDIENTS

- 5 to 7 green frying tomatoes (they are labeled as such in your vegetable section at the grocery store; you should get 3 to 4 slices per tomato)
- 4 eggs, beaten
- 1 pint buttermilk
- 1 15-ounce container of plain breadcrumbs
- 1 2-pound bag of yellow plain cornmeal
- Olive oil
- Smoked paprika
- Sweetener of choice (I like Stevia)
- Salt and pepper

DIRECTIONS

1. Cut tomatoes into ½-inch pieces (approximately 3 slices per tomato). Put slices on a rack to drain, approximately 15 minutes per side. Beat eggs in a dish deep enough to dip the tomatoes. Add milk to beaten eggs. Mix your breadcrumbs and cornmeal in a separate dish with ⅔ being cornmeal. Dip tomatoes in eggs mixture and then dredge in cornmeal and breadcrumb mixture. Use a large frying pan or an electric fryer and heat about ½ inch of oil. Make sure oil is hot enough by testing with a little ball of cornmeal and milk; drop a little in until it sizzles in the pan. Remember, you don't want a thick crust on the tomato, just a light coating. That's the issue I have with fried foods–save the thick crust for fried chicken where it should be.

2. Fry tomatoes in hot oil, about 2 to 3 minutes on each side or until light brown; don't let the slices touch each other, and sprinkle with preferred seasonings. I do a dash of paprika, a dash of sweetener, salt, and pepper. Season each side. When you remove the slices, put them on a wire rack to drain. If you don't have one, you can use your oven rack; just put paper towels under it. I like to taste a tomato and decide if I want more seasonings. (This is the same way I cook fried okra.)

3. For sauce, you have as many options as your mind will let you concoct. Dill, feta cheese, and sour cream make a nice option. Just mix together until you get a flavor that you like. Pimento cheese can also be good. Another option might be mayonnaise and Thousand Island dressing with a bit of red pepper. Create, create!

NOTE: Here's a shocker (fasten your seatbelts–I almost had to pour a grandma shot when I learned this). I was drinking a martini at the time, so that held me together! When I was fine-tuning my recipe, my friends, Mark Corsale and Taylor Boyd, were my sous-chefs, for lack of a better term. We decided to look up the origins of fried green tomatoes. Well, the gods above and the devil below must have gasped as we did! Fried green tomatoes originated in OHIO! That's right! They originated in the Midwest and Northeast and are thought to be linked to the cuisine of Jewish immigrants. It is hilarious when you realize that Southern cities such as Charleston and Savannah and elsewhere sell them by the thousands, and everyone just assumes they are a typical Southern dish. Far from it.

HAMBY'S SHRIMP SALAD

SERVING SIZE: 3 CUPS | **PREP TIME:** 30 MINS | **COOKING TIME:** 3 TO 5 MINS

*M*iss Hamby is known in Charleston for her catering. Hamby's is an institution for sure. They are also known for their shrimp sandwiches—you can always identify Hamby's food at any event. I was creating a menu for my dad's 75th birthday party some years back, and the idea of shrimp sandwiches came up. I looked online, and lo and behold, Miss Hamby's Shrimp Salad, along with other recipes of hers, was just waiting for me on her website. This salad is easy to make, and rather than go to the effort of making small cocktail sandwiches, we served it in a large bowl with crackers as a spread. Well, take a memo: When it's delicious and there is a spoon around, guests tend to serve themselves large spoonfuls rather than bother with crackers! It goes fast!

INGREDIENTS

- 2 ½ pounds cooked shrimp*, coarsely chopped
- 2 ½ teaspoons salt
- 1 teaspoon lemon juice
- 2 tablespoons minced onion
- 1 cup chopped celery
- ½ teaspoon celery seeds
- 1 teaspoon hot sauce, such as Tabasco
- 1 cup mayonnaise (or enough to bind the mixture)

*Hold the shrimp by its tail right where it attaches to the body. Grab about ⅓ down the shrimp with both fingers reaching around, and grab the underside middle of the shrimp. Pinch it there, and that whole section of shell should come right off. Then, pinch the rest gently near the tail and the rest of the meat should slide right out of the tail section. For the record: I do not, nor will I ever, devein my shrimp!

DIRECTIONS

1. In a large bowl, combine shrimp, salt, and lemon juice.

2. Add onions, celery, celery seeds, hot sauce, and mayonnaise. Mix well and refrigerate.

COOK THE SHRIMP

3. Shrimp only take about 2 to 3 minutes to cook. Peel your shrimp and remove the tail. Bring water in a pot to a boil, and add shrimp. Cover and cut the heat off. When the shrimp are pink all the way through, they are done.

NOTE: If you decide to make cocktail sandwiches, cut off the edges of your bread. Then, put a layer of shrimp salad between the slices, and cut the bread in quarters. These can be made the day before and refrigerated. As for mayonnaise, my preference is Duke's! Hellmann's next!

HOT SPINACH CRAB DIP

SERVING SIZE: 6 TO 8 | **PREP TIME:** 15 MINS | **COOKING TIME:** 15 MINS

First, let's talk about an absolutely delicious surprise! Who doesn't like this spinach dip? It's been around since before sliced bread, hasn't it? And who doesn't love crab? I was experimenting one day with my friend, Mary, and we stumbled upon this. Boy, did we create something special. Easy, delicious, and decadent, it needs to be served warm to do it justice. Place it in a chafing dish if you are having a party, and corn scoops are a perfect pairing. Scoop that spinach and crab right up!

INGREDIENTS

- 1 package Knorr Vegetable Recipe Mix
- 1 16-ounce container sour cream
- 1 8-ounce can water chestnuts, diced
- 1 cup mayonnaise
- 3 green onions, chopped fine
- 1 8-ounce can crab meat (lump or claw)
- 1 10-ounce box frozen spinach, thawed

DIRECTIONS

1. Make dip per instructions on the back of the Knorr package.

2. Stir in crab meat.

3. Transfer mixture to a medium soup pot and heat on medium-low until warm.

4. Serve with corn chip scoops.

NOTE: If not using a chafing dish, the dip can be put on warm in a small crock pot. I have even hollowed out a purple cabbage to use as a serving bowl with it.

MARINATED SHRIMP

SERVING SIZE: 6 TO 8 | **PREP TIME:** 24 HRS | **COOKING TIME:** 2 MINS

*I*n Charleston you *must* have different variations of shrimp recipes on hand, as it's so plentiful here. I have served this out of Tupperware at a tailgate party and on a gorgeous tray for an elegant cocktail party. It's always a hit.

INGREDIENTS

- 2 pounds shrimp, cooked and peeled
- 1 16-ounce can black olives, drained
- 1 10-ounce jar green olives, drained
- 1 14-ounce can baby corn, drained
- 1 10-ounce jar whole mushrooms, drained
- 1 small container cherry tomatoes
- 1 16-ounce block sharp cheddar cheese, cubed
- 2 16-ounce bottles Italian dressing
- 1 medium green or red bell pepper, sliced in strips (optional)

DIRECTIONS

1. Combine all ingredients in a large Ziploc bag (or two). Add dressing to each bag enough to cover, and let marinate at least 24 hours in the refrigerator.

2. Drain in colander and put mixture on a serving tray with decorative lettuce. Sprinkle with Nature's Seasoning to taste and serve.

NOTE: This is about as easy as it gets for an impressive appetizer, and there are lots of ways to make it. You can chop the bell pepper for a little more texture and color, or perhaps not use the cheese. Throw a jar of pickled okra in to add a bit of zest! Or, get creative and use two different cheeses! It needs to be made the day ahead, so again, a plus when entertaining. Everyone stands by it at the table when I serve it. Also, you can make it grow in size very easily by doubling any of the ingredients.

OLIVE CHEESE BALL AND SANDWICH SPREAD

| **SERVING SIZE:** 6 TO 8 | **PREP TIME:** 20 MINS |

*W*hen I was a child, my mother made these delicious sandwiches with cream cheese and olives. They were a special treat and were not intended to be a meal. My sister, Debbie, and I loved it when Moma made them. I have no idea where she got the recipe, but as I grew up, I learned that other friends' mothers made them, as well. As I got older and went to receptions and parties, I often found those special sandwich treats served as small cocktail sandwiches, and obviously, as you do, you get creative and turn it into a cheese ball. It's an olive lover's dream!

INGREDIENTS

- 8 ounces cream cheese, softened
- 1 stick (8 tablespoons) butter, softened
- ½ small onion, chopped
- 20 black olives, chopped
- 20 green olives, with or without pimentos, chopped
- 1 cup pecans, chopped

DIRECTIONS

1. In a medium bowl, cream softened cream cheese and butter.

2. Add chopped onions and mix in olives.

3. Roll entire mixture into a ball, then cover in chopped pecans until completely covered. Press pecans into the ball, if necessary.

4. Refrigerate at least 8 to 24 hours before serving. Serve with your favorite crackers. I also surround the ball with black and green olives for presentation, making a complete circle. This can also be used as a sandwich spread.

NOTE: Another great thing: this spread can be made in advance so the day of an event you'll have one less thing to do.

SWEET ONION CHEESE DIP

SERVING SIZE: 6 TO 8 | **PREP TIME:** 15 MINS | **COOKING TIME:** 30 MINS

*T*alk about easy and quick. I make this the day before and refrigerate it, but you can make it 10 minutes before you throw it in the oven. Everyone scarfs this up like there's no tomorrow.

INGREDIENTS

- 2 cups sweet or Vidalia onions, chopped in small pieces
- 2 cups sharp cheddar cheese, grated
- ½ cup Parmesan cheese, grated
- 1 cup mozzarella cheese, grated
- 1 cup mayonnaise
- 1 cup bacon bits or crumbled cooked bacon
- Smoked paprika (optional)

DIRECTIONS

1. Preheat oven to 350 degrees Fahrenheit.

2. In a large bowl, mix all ingredients together. Top with bacon and paprika.

3. Bake for about 30 minutes or until bubbly. Let cool and serve with crackers or scoops.

NOTE: I sometimes put different cheeses in this. It does retain some liquid, which I fish out with a spoon before serving, but bottom line—few ingredients, quick, easy, make in advance, and oh-so-good! This also can be made into a pie by simply using a deep-dish pie crust, pouring the ingredients in, and cooking the same amount of time.

RHETT'S TUSCAN TIMBALES

SERVING SIZE: 24 PIECES | **PREP TIME:** 20 MINS | **COOKING TIME:** 10 MINS

$\mathcal{R}$hett Thurman is a highly acclaimed artist in Charleston. She, her husband Harry, and I attend church together at St. Stephen's Episcopal Church. They are fabulous hosts! It is always a treat to go to their home. This recipe is easy, delicious, elegant, and always a hit. Make them once, and you will be hooked!

INGREDIENTS

- 1 sheet Pepperidge Farm puff pastry
- 4 ounces blue cheese crumbles
- 24 walnuts
- 1 small jar honey

DIRECTIONS

1. Preheat oven to 400 degrees Fahrenheit.

2. Carefully cut 1 sheet Pepperidge Farm puff pastry into 24 small rectangles.

3. Spray a miniature muffin tin pan with cooking spray. Press each rectangle of pastry into the cups and sprinkle with enough blue cheese to partially fill. Place a walnut or 2 on top.

4. Bake for at least 8 to 10 minutes—watch them as they may need more, but you don't want them to burn.

5. When pastry turns light brown, remove from oven and drizzle with honey. Remove from pan and transfer to a serving platter. Serve lightly warm.

SAUSAGE BALLS IN SOUR CREAM AND CHUTNEY

SERVING SIZE: 60 TO 70 BALLS | **PREP TIME:** 35 MINS | **COOKING TIME:** 20 MINS

*T*his recipe came from the book *Catering to Columbia* by Gail Rigby Kennedy. Whether I make 100 or 500, there are never any left. When my niece, Lindsay, got married, my friends and I made 1,000 of them. They are easy, elegant, delicious, and always a hit at my parties. I love when a guest says, "Oh, I will buy beef meatballs at Costco and then add them to the sauce." It just doesn't taste the same unless the meatballs are made from sausage!

INGREDIENTS

- 1 pound hot sausage
- 1 pound mild sausage
- 1 16-ounce container sour cream
- 2 9-ounce bottles Major Grey's Mango Chutney

DIRECTIONS

MAKE THE MEATBALLS

1. Preheat oven to 350 degrees Fahrenheit.

2. In a large mixing bowl, mix hot and mild sausages together. I find this easiest to do by hand. Squeeze through your fingers to mix it well!

3. Make small meatballs (larger than a marble but smaller than a golf ball) and place on a cookie sheet lined with foil.

4. Bake for 20 to 25 minutes or until done.

5. Remove meatballs from pan and let any excess grease drain off.

MAKE THE CHUTNEY

1. While meatballs are cooking, pour sour cream into a medium or large pot to warm.

2. Stir in chutney and mix well.

3. If serving immediately, put the cooked, warm meatballs into the sauce and mix well.

4. Serve hot with toothpicks in a crock pot or chafing dish.

NOTE: I have played with the ratio of chutney and sour cream and have found that I can use less chutney. These meatballs can be made in advance and frozen in Ziploc freezer bags. Thaw, then heat them in the microwave when you need them. Make the sauce the day of and add reheated meatballs. Make sure you have toothpicks, and sometimes you may need a serving spoon. Count on all of them being eaten!

SHRIMP MOLD

SERVING SIZE: 12 TO 15 | **PREP TIME:** 15 MINS | **COOKING TIME:** 10 MINS

Shrimp molds are a Southern thing and definitely a Charleston tradition. There are shrimp mold recipes here, there, and yonder, and they all have the same ingredients; some with more shrimp and veggies, and some with less. With a recipe this popular, I'm not sure who can actually claim the original. They are in book after book with the same name and different chefs claiming it's their recipe. This is always a hit at events, and count on it being cleaned off the serving plate.

INGREDIENTS

- 1 10.75-ounce can condensed tomato soup
- 8 ounces cream cheese, softened
- ½ cup finely chopped celery
- 1 cup mayonnaise
- 1 envelope unflavored gelatin
- ½ cup onions, finely chopped
- ½ cup bell pepper, finely chopped
- 1 pound shrimp, cooked and chopped

DIRECTIONS

1. In a saucepan, heat soup and add cream cheese. Mix until well blended and cheese is melted.

2. Soften gelatin in 2 tablespoons of water (I put it in a coffee cup to mix), then stir into hot soup until completely dissolved.

3. Remove from heat, add mayonnaise, and mix well.

4. Let cool in refrigerator 15 to 20 minutes, then stir in remaining ingredients.

5. Grease a 4-cup plastic or Tupperware mold. I line mine with Saran Wrap. Pour mixture in, cover, and refrigerate overnight.

6. Unmold and serve with Ritz crackers.

NOTE: You can purchase molds on Amazon.

Here's something that might come in handy in the face of an emergency: If the mold breaks when you take it out of the container, put it in a serving bowl, and you have a fabulous shrimp spread! Also, you can dress this mold up on a fancy serving dish, setting it on top of lettuce. Arrange black and green olives and lemon wedges all around it. Sprinkle a touch of smoked paprika, as well. Smoked paprika is a gift from the gods that goes well with and enhances everything. You can also slice in inch-wide pieces and put on a layer of lettuce to serve as an aspic-type salad.

Salads

FROZEN FRUIT SALAD 1 AND 2

SERVING SIZE: 6 | **PREP TIME:** 15 MINS | **COOKING TIME:** 5 MINS

*F*ROZEN FRUIT SALAD? Well, YES! There's bound to be one at some point in every Southerner's life. It's just the same as a Jell-O mold! To be honest, this is more of a dessert to me. Perfect on a hot, sultry, summer day. It is beautiful, indeed, on a piece of lettuce. Serve it as a treat with some leftovers.

INGREDIENTS

FRUIT SALAD 1

- 1 8-ounce can crushed pineapple
- 1 8-ounce bottle maraschino cherries
- 8 ounces cream cheese
- 1 10-ounce bag miniature marshmallows
- 1 cup chopped pecans
- ¾ cup mayonnaise
- 1 cup whipping cream

FRUIT SALAD 2

- 2 boxes peach Jell-O
- 1 8-ounce can crushed pineapple
- 1 8-ounce container Cool Whip
- 2 cups buttermilk
- 1 cup pecans, chopped

DIRECTIONS

FRUIT SALAD 1:

1. In a large bowl, mix all ingredients, including juices, except whipping cream.

2. **MAKE STIFF WHIPPING CREAM**—use your food processor on high, but be careful not to turn it into butter. This is a trick I learned for quick whipping cream. You can also pour the whipping cream into a bowl that has been in the freezer for 15 minutes and beat on high until peaks form.

3. Fold whipped cream into other ingredients, then pour mixture into 8 x 11-inch glass dish. Cover with foil and freeze overnight.

FRUIT SALAD 2:

1. Make Jell-O as directed, then add remaining ingredients.

2. Freeze, covered, overnight.

NOTE: History has it that fruit salad was introduced from England in the early 1900s. I have always associated it with Southern food. It just seems like something everyone's great-aunt or grandmother made!

ARTICHOKE-RICE SALAD

SERVING SIZE: 6 | **PREP TIME:** 15 MINS | **COOKING TIME:** 20 MINS

This salad is delicious and different. It will most certainly be a first for your guests, and they will love it! For the best possible flavor, I like to make it a day in advance and let all the flavors blend.

INGREDIENTS

- 1 6- to 8-ounce box chicken-flavored rice mix
- 4 green onions, sliced thin
- ½ green pepper, chopped
- 12 large pimento-stuffed olives, sliced
- 2 6-ounce jars marinated artichoke hearts
- ¾ teaspoon curry powder
- ⅓ cup mayonnaise

DIRECTIONS

1. Cook rice per package directions, omitting the butter. Then cool in a large bowl.

2. Add onions, pepper, and olives.

3. Drain artichoke hearts, reserving the liquid, and cut them in half. Add hearts to rice mixture.

4. Combine artichoke liquid with curry powder and mayonnaise. Add dressing to rice mixture, and toss. Chill before serving.

BOBBY'S SEAFOOD SALAD

SERVING SIZE: 6 | **PREP TIME:** 30 MINS | **COOKING TIME:** 12 TO 15 MINS

INGREDIENTS

- 2 bay leaves
- 1 tablespoon garlic powder
- 1 to 2 tablespoons Old Bay Seasoning
- 2 pounds raw shrimp, shells and tails on
- 1 16-ounce box medium shell pasta
- 1 bunch celery, chopped
- ½ cup sweet relish
- 1 teaspoon mustard
- ¼ cup Duke's mayonnaise
- 3 eggs, hard-cooked and chopped
- ½ to 1 cup Thousand Island dressing
- 1 6-ounce can black olives, sliced
- 1 6-ounce jar whole small mushrooms
- Smoked paprika to taste

NOTE: You can substitute 1 pound shrimp and 1 pound crab meat for a change or use ½ pound crab meat with the shrimp.

DIRECTIONS

1. Bring water to a boil in a large stock pot. Add the bay leaves, garlic powder, and Old Bay, then add the shrimp. When they turn pink, they are done—usually about 2 to 3 minutes at full boil. You can take one out and cut in half to make sure it's pink all the way through.

2. Remove cooked shrimp from the pot with a spoon and transfer to a bowl, saving the shrimp water. Peel shrimp, discarding shells and tails, and set aside.

3. Boil pasta shells in the shrimp water. Cook pasta shells according to directions on box. Drain pasta, and let cool.

4. Once shells and shrimp are cool, transfer both to a large bowl and add all remaining ingredients. I usually add more sweet pickles and Thousand Island dressing and sometimes a dab more mayonnaise. Taste yours, and add more Old Bay if it suits you. Remember, you can add more of any of the dressing ingredients to change the flavor to suit your desired taste. Each time I make this, it's a little different depending on what I add more of. Refrigerate until ready to serve.

CORNBREAD SALAD

SERVING SIZE: 6 TO 8 | **PREP TIME:** 5 MINS | **COOKING TIME:** 15 TO 20 MINS

*C*ornbread is a staple on most Southern tables. Of course, I cheat by using a quick mix, but trust me, this salad is a treat! I got this recipe years ago from Jean Bing-Zaremba when I was in a group called Folly Beach Friends.

INGREDIENTS

- 1 box Jiffy Cornbread Mix
- 1 medium green or red bell pepper, chopped
- 1 medium onion, chopped
- 5 ripe red tomatoes, chopped
- 1 pound bacon, fried and crumbled (substitute ½ to 2 cups bacon bits)
- 1 ½ to 2 cups mayonnaise (I use Duke's)
- 1 to 2 teaspoons sugar
- ½ cup sweet salad dill pickle relish or cubes

DIRECTIONS

1. Prepare cornbread as directed on box. Let cool. Crumble ½ of baked cornbread into a salad bowl or 9 x 13-inch dish.

2. Layer bell pepper, onion, tomatoes, and crumbled bacon. Save enough bacon to sprinkle on top.

3. Mix mayonnaise, sugar, and pickles. Spread mixture on top of bacon. Crumble remaining cornbread on top and sprinkle with remaining bacon. Salad can be made a few hours ahead of the meal. Refrigerate until ready to serve.

NOTE: There is a quick fix to having cooked bacon on hand if you do not want to use the bacon crumbles from your local wholesale store: Preheat your oven to 400 degrees Fahrenheit. Line a cookie sheet with tin foil and lay out a pound of bacon, usually about 8 strips, on the pan. Bake for about 20 minutes or until bacon is crispy. Easy cleanup and no mess on your stovetop. Break the bacon pieces in half, put in a freezer bag, and freeze until needed. Saves a lot of time when preparing. (My niece, Lindsay Pennell, shared this shortcut with me!)

FOYER GROUP SALAD

| **SERVING SIZE:** 6 | **PREP TIME:** 15 MINS |

*M*y friend from church, Virginia Runge, brought this to one of our church foyer dinners, and I had to have the recipe. This is just totally scrumptious, tasty, and one of my all-time favorites. It's always a hit with not a morsel ever left.

INGREDIENTS

- 2 cups iceberg lettuce, torn into small pieces
- 2 cups Romain lettuce, torn
- 6 tablespoons mayonnaise
- 1 small red onion, sliced thin
- 1 cup Swiss cheese, julienned
- 2 cups curly endive, torn into pieces
- 1 ½ cups petite peas
- 8 slices cooked bacon, crumbled
- Salt, pepper, and sugar to taste

DIRECTIONS

1. Place ⅓ of the salad greens into a bowl. Dot with several dollops of mayonnaise and top with ⅓ of the onion. Sprinkle with about ½ to 1 teaspoon sugar and a dash of salt and pepper. Add ⅓ of the peas and ⅓ of the cheese.

2. Repeat layers twice, seasoning each time. **DO NOT TOSS.**

3. Cover and chill at least 2 hours.

4. Just before serving, sprinkle with bacon crumbles and toss.

NOTE: I estimated a good handful of greens for each serving and one slice of bacon per person. A flavorful trick from Virginia is soaking the red onion slices in cold water with about a tablespoon of baking soda for about 15 to 20 minutes. Rinse and dry well before adding to the salad.

BUTTER BEAN SALAD

SERVING SIZE: 6 | **PREP TIME:** 15 MINS | **COOKING TIME:** 10 MINS

This recipe came from my friend, Sandy Streater, in Savannah, Georgia. It was his grandmother's, so the measurements are approximate. This is such a delicious and different salad. It goes with anything you are serving and really dresses up the table, as it's so colorful. I make it the day before and let the flavors mix.

INGREDIENTS

- 2 9-ounce boxes frozen butter beans
- 2 15.5-ounce cans sweet white corn, drained
- 1 bunch green onions, green and white parts only, sliced thin
- 2 to 4 bunches fresh dill, chopped (approximately 3 to 4 tablespoons, or to taste)
- ½ cup sour cream
- ½ cup mayonnaise
- Salt and pepper to taste

DIRECTIONS

1. Cook butter beans per directions on the box. Important: DO NOT OVERCOOK BUTTER BEANS! Immediately drain and transfer to a bowl of ice water to stop the cooking. Don't leave butter beans in ice water too long–just let them cool.

2. When butter beans are cool, mix with corn in a bowl. Add onions and dill.

3. In a separate small dish, combine sour cream and mayonnaise.

4. Fold sour cream and mayonnaise mixture into butter beans. Add salt and pepper to taste (go easy on the salt).

NOTE: I am a dill lover and always add more to suit my taste buds!

MARINATED SALAD

| **SERVING SIZE:** 6 TO 8 | **PREP TIME:** 15 MINS | **COOKING TIME:** 5 MINS |

This salad is so simple and delicious; everyone always asks for the recipe. This can be made in advance and goes with any meat dish.

INGREDIENTS

- 1 16-ounce can French green beans
- 1 12-ounce can shoepeg white corn
- 1 17-ounce can petite peas
- 1 14-ounce can artichoke hearts
- 1 2-ounce jar pimentos
- 1 4.5-ounce can mushrooms, pieces and stems
- 1 small onion, chopped fine
- 1 green bell pepper, chopped fine

MARINADE

- ½ cup salad oil
- 1 cup dark cider vinegar
- 1 cup sugar

DIRECTIONS

1. Drain veggies well and put in a container with a lid.

2. In a small saucepan, heat salad oil and vinegar on low. Slowly pour in sugar and stir until well mixed. Let cool.

3. Pour marinade over veggies and chill in refrigerator, covered, overnight.

Main Entrees

BOBBY'S LOWCOUNTRY SHRIMP AND GRITS

| **SERVING SIZE:** 4 TO 6 | **PREP TIME:** 15 MINS | **COOKING TIME:** 20 MINS |

Shrimp and grits! Oh yeah, baby. There are dozens of different recipes out there, but as far as I'm concerned, it's all about the flavor of the gravy and the amount of shrimp you have. I have made several versions, and this one breaks the mold. It was so good I ate most of it right out of the pan when I created it. The Old Bay and the sausage add just the right amount of spice.

INGREDIENTS

- 7 ounces pecan-smoked Andouille sausage, sliced in ¼-inch coins
- 1 tablespoon Old Bay Seasoning
- ½ medium onion, chopped
- ½ green bell pepper, chopped
- 2 to 3 cloves garlic, minced
- 1 medium tomato, diced
- 2 cups seafood stock
- 2 tablespoons all-purpose flour
- 1 cup heavy cream
- 1 ½ pounds of raw shrimp, peeled and tails removed

DIRECTIONS

1. In a large skillet, cook your sausage coins in olive oil until brown around the edges. Add 1 tablespoon Old Bay while browning. Transfer sausage to a paper towel-lined plate to drain, but leave the drippings.

2. Add your onion, bell pepper, garlic, tomato, and 1 ½ cups of your seafood stock and bring to a boil. Simmer, covered, until tender, about 15 min.

3. Add flour to thicken. (I find it easier to transfer some of the liquid to a coffee mug and add 1 tablespoon of flour, mix well, and add it back to the skillet. Increase flour for a thicker consistency.)

4. Add remaining ½ cup seafood stock, heavy cream, and another ½ teaspoon Old Bay. Mix well and let simmer on low for about 5 minutes.

5. Add raw shrimp and put the lid on. Shrimp are cooked when pink throughout.

6. Stir mixture well and serve over grits.

NOTE: Depending on your taste, you may want to add more Old Bay.

BEEF ROAST

| **SERVING SIZE:** 6 TO 8 | **PREP TIME:** 15 MINS | **COOKING TIME:** 8 HRS |

*M*y friend, Pam Middleton Hennet, gave me this recipe. Pam and I graduated from high school together. My grandparents knew her grandparents, and my grandfather taught her mother and sister in school. Our families both go back to Captain Robert Seabrook in Charleston, South Carolina, in 1680! Family connections aside, the great thing about this recipe is that it is easy, delicious, and will be waiting on you at the end of the day. Also, it freezes well.

INGREDIENTS

- Salt and pepper
- 1 beef roast, 3 to 4 pounds
- 3 to 5 tablespoons olive oil (enough to cover the bottom of a large skillet)
- 4 to 6 (or more) potatoes, preferably white or gold, peeled and quartered
- 1 medium onion, sliced
- 2 10.5-ounce cans cream of mushroom soup
- 1 package Lipton onion soup mix
- 1 can (from soup) milk
- 1 small bag baby carrots

DIRECTIONS

1. Salt and pepper meat all over. Brown roast in olive oil on all sides in a large skillet. Transfer meat to a large crock pot and add potatoes, arranging them around roast. Add sliced onion.

2. In a separate bowl, combine cream of mushroom soup, Lipton onion soup mix, and milk (fill one of the soup cans with the milk to measure). Add to crock pot.

3. Cook on low for 8 hours. About 2 hours in, if you are home, add the carrots. If not, a quick fix would be to add a 14 ½-ounce can of cooked carrots 10 minutes before serving. Add salt and pepper to taste. Serve hot over white rice.

NOTE: I cook my white rice in a Charleston Rice Steamer. Always perfect every time. If you don't have a steamer, Google it and buy one, as a couple of my recipes call for it.

BEEF TENDERLOIN

SERVING SIZE: 6 | **PREP TIME:** 10 MINS | **COOKING TIME:** 45 MINS

*T*his roast is so delicious and a definite winner every time. I pair it with my Bourbon Carrots and Sweet and Sour Green Beans.

INGREDIENTS

- 5 to 6 pounds beef tenderloin
- 1 ½ to 2 sticks (12 tablespoons plus) butter
- 4 to 6 cloves garlic, crushed
- 1 tablespoon Worcestershire sauce
- 1 tablespoon lemon juice
- Salt to taste
- Ground pepper to taste (but you'll want to use a lot of it!)

DIRECTIONS

1. Preheat oven to 500 degrees Fahrenheit.

2. Allow tenderloin to come to room temperature. In a medium bowl, combine softened butter, crushed garlic, Worcestershire sauce, lemon juice, salt, and pepper. Spread butter mixture on tenderloin.

3. Roast, uncovered, on a baking sheet for 23 minutes. Remove from oven, wrap meat in foil, and allow to rest for 20 minutes. Remove foil immediately after resting to discontinue cooking.

NOTE: Do not scrimp on the butter mixture. Sometimes I add more and make sure the meat is just lathered down with it. This statement is for the over 18 crowd, but my stepsister and I dubbed this "sex in your mouth!"

DONA'S STEAK SAUCE

SERVING SIZE: ENOUGH FOR 4 STEAKS | **PREP TIME:** 5 MINS | **COOKING TIME:** 5 MINS

This sauce is great on steaks and other beef dishes. I got it from my good friends, Tommy and Kim Brush. Dona was Tommy's mother. Honestly, this is so good–better than any store-bought meat sauce.

INGREDIENTS

- 4 tablespoons butter
- ½ teaspoon dry mustard
- 2 tablespoons soy sauce
- 1 teaspoon fresh parsley, minced
- 1 tablespoon ketchup
- 1 teaspoon lemon juice
- Dash black pepper

DIRECTIONS

1. Mix all ingredients well over low heat. Serve warm.

NOTE: You may want to double this!

CHICKEN BOG

SERVING SIZE: 6 | **PREP TIME:** 30 MINS | **COOKING TIME:** 30 MINS

*C*hicken Bog is a Lowcountry dish, and history has it that it came from the Pee Dee area north of Charleston, originating in the 1800s. The recipe has changed and has some different variations. I love it because I can get creative. Sometimes I add bulk sausage that has been browned. At one dinner, I added sausage, a pound of bacon, and a pound of shrimp that had been cooked in the bacon grease! You can bet everyone thought they were in high cotton! Just in case you did not know, "high cotton" means you are in the upper echelons.

INGREDIENTS

- 1 whole cooked chicken
- 1 pound hot sausage
- 1 large Vidalia or sweet onion, chopped
- 1 bunch celery, chopped
- 1 small (6-ounce) or large (13.25-ounce) can mushrooms
- 2 8-ounce cans diced water chestnuts
- 2 cups cooked white rice
- 1 to 3 cups canned chicken broth
- Poultry seasoning
- Salt and pepper
- Nature's Seasoning
- Smoked paprika to taste

NOTE: I have an electric smoker, and there's nothing better than a home-smoked chicken or turkey in this bog. This makes a hearty meal—all you need to do is add salad and bread. I buy cooked chickens from the grocery store, debone them, and put the meat in freezer bags so I always have cooked chicken on hand if I need it.

DIRECTIONS

1. Pull all meat off the chicken and set aside.

2. In a large skillet, fry sausage, breaking it into small pieces. Transfer to a paper towel-lined plate and set aside to drain.

3. Sauté onions and celery on low in grease from sausage. You may have to add a splash or 2 of olive oil, or better yet, a nice pat of butter.

4. Transfer mixture to a large bowl. Slowly add cooked rice, and mix well, including any juices and drippings.

5. Slowly add chicken broth and mix well. You may not use all of the broth; the mixture should be wet, but not mushy.

6. Add all seasonings to taste. Remember, you are in control of the flavor. Taste as you cook, adding to your liking.

7. Place mixture in large baking pan and cover with tinfoil.

NOTE: If serving later, reheat at 350 degrees Fahrenheit until warm.

FROGMORE STEW

| **SERVING SIZE:** 6 | **PREP TIME:** 15 MINS | **COOKING TIME:** 30 MINS |

*F*rogmore Stew is the basis for Beaufort Stew, Lowcountry Boil, and anything else anyone is trying to call this mixture. It is a classic Lowcountry dish here in Charleston and is served in most restaurants. Everyone knows this dish well. What most don't know is that it originated from Frogmore, South Carolina. Frogmore is a spot—and I mean if you blink, you will miss it—between Beaufort, South Carolina, and Fripp Island. Many years ago, regular folk would cook what they had on hand to eat. They lived in the country on the salt waterways. Think about it: What did they have? Fresh seafood, corn, and potatoes. Sausage was easy enough to have on hand. They learned to boil this mixture, sometimes adding fresh blue crabs to it.

INGREDIENTS

- 2 pounds shrimp, peeled and tails removed
- 6 ears of corn, shucked, cleaned, and broken in half
- 2 13-ounce packs of kielbasa or smoked turkey sausage, sliced into 1-inch chunks
- 8 medium potatoes, cleaned, skin intact, and cut in half
- 1 12-ounce can of any regular flavored beer
- 2 sticks (16 tablespoons) butter, divided
- Old Bay Seasoning
- Nature's Seasoning

DIRECTIONS

1. Prep your ingredients the day before to make it easier: Peel shrimp, cover with water, and refrigerate in a lidded container. Clean and break your corn and refrigerate in a large Ziploc bag. Slice your sausage and refrigerate in a second large Ziploc bag. Do the same with your potatoes.

2. Pull out your biggest pot and fill it about ⅔ full with water. Pour in the beer, and drop in 1 stick (8 tablespoons) butter. Pour in at least ¼ cup Old Bay Seasoning. (You may want to add more Old Bay. This is up to you and your tastes.) Bring to a boil.

3. Add your potatoes first and cook for about 5 to 8 minutes. Check to make sure they have started to get tender.

4. Add the sausage. Keep at high heat. Cook the sausage about 5 minutes and check the potatoes again. You don't want them to get too mushy.

5. Add your corn and cook for about 3 to 5 minutes (I like my corn cooked, but crunchy). You do not want to overcook the corn.

6. Turn heat off and add shrimp; stir. Put the lid on, give it about 3 minutes, and then check it. If shrimp are pink all the way through, they are done. Doesn't take a shrimp but 2 or 3 minutes to cook in boiling water.

7. Remove about a cup of broth and set aside. Drain the entire pot into a large colander. Once most of the broth has dripped off and while ingredients are still hot, transfer all to a large platter or even a large baking pan, depending on how you will be serving.

8. Pour the reserved broth over the stew and slice up the second stick (8 tablespoons) of butter. Drop slices evenly over hot stew and lightly sprinkle with Old Bay and Nature's Seasoning to taste.

NOTE: You cannot go wrong with measurements. Just don't overcook anything. The more you make this, the more you will fine tune it to your tastes. I have no idea why they call it a stew because once the liquid is poured out, it is NOT a stew. Now, about the shrimp—I am the ONLY person I know who always peels the shrimp in every dish I make, and I remove the tails. I don't think my guests should have to peel their own shrimp, especially at the table. The tail thing blows my mind. All the fancy restaurants, and the not-so-fancy, leave the tails on in many of their dishes involving shrimp. Drives me insane! Who wants to be eating shrimp and grits and then have to put your finger in the dish to remove the tails? The local chefs say leaving the tail on is for presentation. Well, just let me make it clear, that will NEVER happen at my house!

LEMON CHICKEN

SERVING SIZE: 6 | **PREP TIME:** 20 MINS | **COOKING TIME:** 25 MINS

INGREDIENTS

- 1 whole cooked chicken, meat removed from bone
- Lemon pepper
- Olive oil
- 2 cups cream or milk (more may be needed)
- 1 10-ounce can condensed cream of chicken soup
- 1 13.25-ounce can mushrooms, stems and pieces
- 1 8-ounce can diced water chestnuts
- 2 lemons
- 1 12-ounce bag egg noodles
- 1 pound shrimp, peeled, tails removed (optional)

DIRECTIONS

1. Break chicken meat into bite-size pieces. Sauté in lemon pepper and olive oil on low heat in a large skillet. Use just enough oil to coat the chicken pieces. Use your judgment, but it's usually a few tablespoons. I am a taster, so sprinkle a bit of lemon pepper to start and see how you feel about the flavor. Then decide if you will add more.

2. Pour enough milk or cream to cover the meat halfway. Add soup and blend well. You may need to add more milk, depending on your pan. If you want a thicker sauce, add another can of soup.

3. Add water chestnuts and mushrooms. Mix well and keep on low to medium heat. Taste the broth again, and season to taste.

4. Boil egg noodles in a large pot and drain well. I have mixed it all together and sprinkled it with Parmesan cheese or will let each guest serve their own.

NOTE: For a special treat, add a pound of shrimp. You can bring the mixture to a boil, add the shrimp, and put the lid on. Shrimp only take about 2 to 3 minutes to cook. They are done when they're pink all the way through. The smaller the shrimp, the sweeter the flavor, and I always remove the tails. Squeeze some fresh lemon juice in, of course, or a squirt or two from a bottle. If you want your sauce to be thicker, transfer some to a coffee mug or small dish. Add 1 tablespoon flour, mix well, then pour that mixture back into the pan. Mix well to see how much it thickens it. If you want it thicker, repeat the flour.

LOWCOUNTRY SHRIMP AND SAUSAGE CASSEROLE

SERVING SIZE: 6 TO 8 | **PREP TIME:** 15 MINS | **COOKING TIME:** 30 MINS

*T*his is one of my signature dishes. I created it from my shrimp soup, which is also a signature dish. It's one of those dishes where guests get up on their own for seconds. I have even seen thirds. It's impressive, delicious, and can be served at the fanciest of tables or in the kitchen at the breakfast bar.

INGREDIENTS

- 2 6.2-ounce boxes wild rice
- 1 pound hot Jimmy Dean sausage
- 1 red bell pepper, chopped
- 1 large green pepper, chopped
- 1 large Vidalia onion, chopped
- Old Bay Seasoning
- 2 pounds shrimp, peeled and cooked
- 1 12-ounce can sliced mushrooms, drained
- 2 8-ounce cans diced water chestnuts, drained
- 2 10-ounce cans condensed cream of shrimp soup
- 2 2-ounce bags almond slivers

DIRECTIONS

1. Start your rice according to the package directions. While it is cooking, use a large skillet or frying pan to cook your sausage, breaking it into small pieces. Once browned, transfer sausage to a paper towel-lined plate, leaving grease in pan.

2. Sauté your bell peppers and onion in the sausage drippings and add a few heavy sprinkles of Old Bay Seasoning, giving the vegetables a good coat. If the pan is getting dry, you may have to add a little olive oil, but don't let your veggies burn. Cook until veggies are tender.

3. Add your shrimp while your veggies are still cooking, and stir around until they turn pink. Pull one out and cut it in half. If it's pink all the way through, it's done.

4. Add your mushrooms and water chestnuts. Add some more Old Bay—a good dash or two.

5. Combine cooked rice, shrimp mixture, sausage, and one can of soup in a large bowl. Mix well and yes, taste it! You don't want it too soupy, and one can may give it all the flavor it needs. You may think another dash of Old Bay might be good. As mentioned, I like to put a few spoonfuls into a coffee mug and sample it. Yes, I eat out of the pan . . . who doesn't? It's quite acceptable when tasting!

6. Put the mixture in a 9 x 12-inch baking dish that has been sprayed with your preferred cooking spray. Sprinkle the top with almonds. If it is still hot and close to dinner time, cover with tin foil, and you are ready to go.

NOTE: I always make this a day ahead and leave it in the frying pan to heat up the day of. All you need is a salad and bread, and you are set. This is one of my go-to dishes. I will pull an appetizer and desert out of the freezer the day before. A good match with this is the Smoked Oyster Cream Cheese Curry Ball or Liver Pâté and my Chocolate Pie. You could make my Beer Loaf with this, too.

MEDITERRANEAN SHRIMP

SERVING SIZE: 6 | **PREP TIME:** 30 MINS | **COOKING TIME:** 20 MINS

There's a funny story about how this dish came about. It has become another one of my signature dishes, yet I have no idea how I initially made it. I suffer from insomnia at times, and I often have to take Ambien. Well, apparently, I made this on Ambien one night in my sleep and then posted it as my new shrimp dish on Facebook at 3 a.m. When I woke up that morning, I was scrolling through Facebook and saw MY new dish! I was horrified and ran to the kitchen to see every ingredient all over the counters and the dish itself wrapped up tightly in a large cast iron skillet in the refrigerator. It tasted DELICIOUS! So, I recreated it. It's so colorful that I named it Mediterranean Shrimp. Perhaps I should rename it Sleepwalking Shrimp!

INGREDIENTS

- Olive oil
- 1 large red bell pepper, chopped
- 1 large orange bell pepper, chopped
- 1 large yellow bell pepper, chopped
- Smoked paprika
- 1 14-ounce can baby corn, chopped in thirds
- 1 16-ounce can large black olives, sliced in half
- 1 10-ounce jar large green olives, sliced in half
- 1 8-ounce can diced water chestnuts
- 4 cups chicken broth
- 1 pint heavy cream
- 2 pounds cooked shrimp, peeled
- Pepper
- Nature's Seasoning

DIRECTIONS

1. Sauté bell peppers in olive oil until tender, usually about 10 minutes. Stir constantly so they don't burn, adding several shakes of smoked paprika. I am pretty heavy with it.

2. Once peppers are tender, add chopped baby corn, sliced olives, and water chestnuts. Add chicken broth and heavy cream, and bring to a boil and let simmer.

3. Drop the shrimp in at the end, as they only need to cook about 2 minutes until they are pink all the way through. The mixture should be a gorgeous orange-rust color from the paprika. Add more paprika and Nature's Seasoning to taste. Serve over yellow rice. Makes a beautiful dish. As with most of my recipes, I want to teach my readers to cook to THEIR tastes. Add the seasonings along the way and test the flavor.

MOMS' SUNDAY POT ROAST

| **SERVING SIZE:** 4 TO 6 | **PREP TIME:** 20 MINS | **COOKING TIME:** 5 HRS |

*M*oms was my daddy's mother. She was 44 when I was born, and we were inseparable. She was one of the most influential people in my life, always young and always beautiful. We rotated Sunday dinner between my grandparents' house and my parents'. They were only about a smidgen of a mile apart, a 5-minute walk. Moms often cooked this pot roast and a cake, and Moma made the side vegetables. Moms would also make white rice in the oven, which I loved 'cause the sides were so crispy.

INGREDIENTS

- 1 3- to 4-pound bone-in Angus beef pot roast
- 1 10.5-ounce can condensed French onion soup
- ½ cup red wine
- 1 7 ounce package dry Italian dressing
- Salt and pepper
- Nature's Seasoning

NOTE: Sunday dinner was a big deal in my family. Keep in mind, dinner is lunch and supper is the evening meal. My funniest story about Moms was that she told me never to eat after someone else because they had germs and I might catch something. One day, she cooked a hamburger and asked me if I wanted a bite. I replied, "Moms, you said never to eat after anyone that I might catch something." She replied "Darling, it's okay, we don't have germs!"

Moms' roast is great with Bourbon Carrots, Sweet and Sour Green Beans, Beer Bread, and Peach Chiffon Pie. Or, add some of Jesse's Southern Bacon Gravy you pulled out the freezer to the drippings and fix a pot of rice.

DIRECTIONS

1. Preheat oven to 275 degrees Fahrenheit.

2. Put roast in a large roasting pan. Mine is 17 x 13.5 inches.

3. Pour all remaining ingredients over the roast. Add Nature's Seasoning, salt, and pepper to taste. Cover roast tightly with tin foil and cook at least 5 hours.

4. Check for tenderness at 5 hours. I like my meat falling off the bone, so it may need to cook a little longer, depending on your stove. Check after a couple of hours to make sure your liquid is not evaporating. If it is evaporating, just add some water or more soup. Once it is cooked, you might add a can of beef broth and flour to make a good gravy. First mix a couple of teaspoons of flour in a cup with the broth and then pour it into the pan to thicken.

OKRA, SHRIMP, SAUSAGE, AND CHICKEN GUMBO

| **SERVING SIZE:** 8 TO 10 | **PREP TIME:** 20 MINS | **COOKING TIME:** 30 TO 40 MINS |

This is cheating big time, but you will absolutely LOVE the flavor of this gumbo. A very close friend of mine, Sara Marsha Rafter, is a fabulous cook and entertains at a professional level. Every time she serves gumbo, everyone rants and raves, so I pulled her aside one night and asked what her secret was to her delicious roux. She smiled and confessed she bought the dry mix in a country store. I went on Amazon that night and lo and behold, there it was. I bought six bags. You can get creative and make it a shrimp or seafood gumbo, or an okra and sausage gumbo, or a chicken gumbo. You get the idea. Experiment with different sausages, too.

INGREDIENTS

- 4 cups water
- 4 cups chicken broth
- 1 8-ounce bag Country Store Home Style Soup Mix (Louisiana Style Gumbo, or your favorite dry gumbo mix)
- 1 28-ounce bag frozen cut okra
- 1 13-ounce pack smoked turkey sausage, sliced into ¼-inch thick coins
- 1 whole cooked chicken, deboned
- 1 to 2 pounds shrimp, peeled and tails removed
- Zatarain's Pure Ground Gumbo Filé
- Old Bay Seasoning

DIRECTIONS

1. Bring water and broth to a boil, and add all ingredients except shrimp. Let simmer for about 30 minutes and check the tenderness of the okra.

2. Throw a few shakes of the Gumbo Filé in to start, taste, and add it along with Old Bay Seasoning to suit your own tastes.

3. When okra is tender, add the shrimp, put a lid on, and cut off the heat. Stir every couple of minutes, and when shrimp are pink all the way through, they are done. Serve over rice. This is great with my Beer Loaf.

NOTE: I served this at my annual tree trimming party, and everyone gobbled it up. It's just so rich and delicious. Okra should be in this, but if you omit it, I think it should be called a stew. This dish is easy to make: no all-day cooking as you would expect with developing the base and the roux.

Buy your cooked chicken at the grocery store. I usually buy two, debone them, and freeze the meat in a freezer bag to pull out when I might need it.

There is a dispute over whether gumbo originated in Louisiana or Charleston. Of course, I vote for Charleston. Either way, it goes back to at least the 1800s, if not earlier, and was a dish the slaves brought with them from Africa. It is from the Gullah Geechee culture.

PEPPER STEAK

| **SERVING SIZE:** 4 | **PREP TIME:** 15 MINS | **COOKING TIME:** 1 HR |

I first had this when my step-mother, Lorraine, made it. I went back for thirds! It's one of those dishes you can make on Sunday, and it's waiting for you when you get home Monday from work. Add a salad and a loaf of bread, and you have dinner. Serve over white rice. It's definitely company-worthy, and a nice red wine goes well with it, too.

INGREDIENTS

- 2 pounds sirloin, cut in thin strips
- ⅓ cup salad oil
- 1 ¼ teaspoon salt
- ¼ teaspoon pepper
- 2 10.5-ounce cans beef broth
- Garlic, to taste
- 3 medium green peppers
- ½ cup chopped onions
- 1/3 cup cornstarch
- 1 teaspoon soy sauce
- 1 4-ounce can mushrooms
- ¼ cup water
- 2 cups cherry tomatoes, halved

DIRECTIONS

1. In a large skillet, brown sirloin in oil. Stir in salt, pepper, garlic, and broth. Cover and simmer until meat is tender—about 20 to 30 minutes.

2. Stir in green peppers and onions. Cook until tender.

3. In a small bowl, mix cornstarch and water, stirring well to remove all lumps. Add soy sauce, and pour into meat mixture.

4. Add tomatoes and mushrooms and simmer 20 to 30 minutes.

SHRIMP SOUP

SERVING SIZE: 6 | **PREP TIME:** 15 MINS | **COOKING TIME:** 20 TO 30 MINS

This is another one of my signature dishes. I have added crumbled (cooked) sausage and a can of crab meat, which makes for a very decadent dish. No matter what, it is always a hit, though oddly enough, it started out as a dip and ended up as a soup.

INGREDIENTS

- Olive oil
- 1 or 2 large Vidalia onions
- 1 large red bell pepper
- 1 large green bell pepper
- 1 large yellow bell pepper
- Old Bay Seasoning
- 1 quart half and half
- 6 10.5-ounce cans of cream of shrimp soup
- 1 8-ounce can diced water chestnuts
- 2 pounds raw shrimp, peeled, tails removed
- Cooked sausage (optional)
- Canned or fresh crab (optional)

DIRECTIONS

1. Sauté onions and bell peppers in olive oil until tender, about 10 minutes. Sprinkle heavily with Old Bay Seasoning, lightly coating the vegetables.

2. Add half and half and mix well. Add soup one can at a time, and blend well after each addition. Mix well and keep on low heat.

3. Add water chestnuts. Taste soup mixture and season to taste with more Old Bay. I usually put a little soup in a small bowl or coffee mug and experiment with the flavor.

4. After you achieve the flavor you are looking for, add the shrimp. Cover and cook 2 to 3 minutes or until shrimp turn pink.

5. Serve over white rice and keep a bowl of Old Bay on the table for adding sprinkles.

TERRACE SHRIMP CREOLE

| **SERVING SIZE:** 6 | **PREP TIME:** 15 MINS | **COOKING TIME:** 30 TO 45 MINS |

In the old days, we thought that to get a delicious tasting creole, we had to let it simmer for hours the day before and let all the flavors mix. This recipe proves that theory wrong. This one's delicious, and your guests will be going back for seconds.

INGREDIENTS

- 8 slices cooked bacon, crumbled
- 1 cup chopped green bell pepper
- 1 cup chopped onion
- 1 cup chopped celery
- 4 to 6 cloves garlic, minced
- Olive oil or butter
- 2 tablespoons+ Old Bay Seasoning
- ¼ to ½ tablespoon sugar substitute (I like Stevia.)
- Salt and pepper
- 2 12-ounce cans diced tomatoes
- 2 pounds raw shrimp, peeled and tails removed
- Nature's Seasoning

DIRECTIONS

1. In a large skillet, cook bacon and set aside, leaving grease in pan.

2. Sauté next 4 ingredients in olive oil and butter until tender, about 10 minutes. I use enough olive oil to cover the bottom of the skillet, an 8-ounce stick of butter, or a combination of both.

3. Add bacon, then 2 tablespoons Old Bay, sugar substitute, and some salt and pepper.

4. Once tender, add diced tomatoes.

5. Mix all together and bring to a boil.

6. Cut the heat off, add the shrimp, mix well, and put the top on the pan. Check it after a few minutes and stir shrimp in until they are pink all the way through. At this point, I taste to see how I like the flavor. I might add a half pack of sugar substitute or some more Old Bay. I like mine a little spicy from the Old Bay but with a hint of sweetness. Add Nature's Seasoning to taste.

7. Serve over white rice.

THE BEST BOSTON BUTT

| **SERVING SIZE:** 6 TO 8 | **PREP TIME:** 15 MINS | **COOKING TIME:** 8 TO 10 HRS |

The name for this cut of meat is said to have come from New England. Throughout the American Revolutionary War, New England butchers tended to take less-prized cuts of pork, like hams and shoulders, and pack them into barrels for storage and transport, known as a butt, which comes from the Latin word "buttis," meaning cask or barrel.

INGREDIENTS

- 1 4- to 5-pound Boston butt or pork shoulder
- Oil for frying
- 1 ½ cups white cider vinegar
- 1 cup firmly packed brown sugar
- 1 tablespoon smoked paprika
- ½ tablespoon salt
- Black pepper to taste
- ½ to 1 teaspoon cayenne pepper

DIRECTIONS

1. Brown your butt in some oil in a frying pan, then put it into a crock pot.

2. Combine remaining ingredients in a large measuring cup, then pour over the butt and cook on low for 8 to 10 hours.

3. Check at 8 hours, and if it's not falling apart, cook it longer.

4. Let it cool in order for the fat to separate. Once cooled, skim the fat off the top while still in the crock pot. Remove meat from crock pot, leaving the liquid.

5. Shred the meat, then put it back in the liquid and reheat. At this point, I taste the liquid to see if I want to make it sweeter with more brown sugar or spicier with more cayenne pepper.

NOTE: If you want to turn this into BBQ, remove liquid from crock pot, pour a bottle of your favorite BBQ sauce on top, and mix well. Great thing about this is, yes, oh yes, you can make it in advance and store it in freezer bags to be pulled out when you want it. Add the BBQ sauce after. Also, remember: We all have different tastes. I, for one, do not like it so spicy that you lose the flavor of what you are actually eating. You can adjust black pepper and cayenne pepper to your liking.

This is easy to make and works great for a crowd when serving other dishes.

Sides

VEGETABLE CASSEROLE

SERVING SIZE: 6 TO 8 | **PREP TIME:** 15 MINS | **COOKING TIME:** 30 TO 45 MINS

INGREDIENTS

- 1 15-ounce can small peas, drained
- 1 7-ounce can shoepeg corn, drained
- 1 14.5-ounce can French style green beans, drained
- 1 10.5-ounce can condensed cream of celery soup
- 1 can diced water chestnuts
- ½ cup onion, chopped
- ½ cup celery, chopped
- ½ cup sour cream
- ¾ cup grated sharp cheddar cheese, grated
- 1 3-ounce bag sliced almonds
- ½ to 1 stick (4 to 8 tablespoons) butter, melted
- 1 large sleeve of Ritz crackers, crushed

DIRECTIONS

1. Preheat oven to 350 degrees Fahrenheit.

2. In a large bowl, combine canned vegetables, soup, water chestnuts, onions, celery, sour cream, and cheese.

3. Spray a 2-quart casserole dish with nonstick vegetable oil and pour mixture into it.

4. Add a few dashes of salt and pepper or Nature's Seasoning.

5. Add crushed crackers and sprinkle sliced almonds on top.

6. Drizzle with melted butter and bake for 30 to 45 minutes, or when crackers are browning and mixture is bubbling around the edges.

NOTE: I once substituted walnuts for the almonds, and that was different and went well.

ADAM'S RUN BUTTER BEANS

SERVING SIZE: 6 TO 8 | **PREP TIME:** 15 MINS | **COOKING TIME:** 30 MINS

*B*utter beans, as lima beans are called in the South, are a Southern staple. We used to think we could only cook them in the summer when they were fresh or if your grandmother froze them. Now you can grab them frozen at the grocery store any season of the year! These butter beans are delicious with chicken, ham, or beef. Many Southerners, including yours truly, eat them over white rice. My cousin, Rose Anne Baldwin, makes wonderful butter beans, so I took her idea and ran with it. Rose Anne lives in our great-grandmother Naomi Baily Welch's house in Adam's Run, a small village about 35 miles south of Charleston. As a child, no matter when I went to see "Mama," she always had something cooking, usually butter beans and rice.

INGREDIENTS

- 4 10-ounce bags frozen Ford Hook Lima Beans (thawed)
- 6 strips bacon
- 6 cups chicken broth
- 1 to 2 teaspoons preferred sweetener (I like Stevia.)
- Salt and pepper (I tend to go heavy on the pepper.)
- Dash Nature's Seasoning

DIRECTIONS

1. Cut your bacon in quarters. Brown bacon in the bottom of a large soup pot. Add chicken broth and bring to a boil.

2. Add your beans and flavor with salt and pepper to taste.

3. Cut down the heat and put a lid on the pot. Let simmer about 20 minutes. Check the beans to see if they are getting soft. You don't want them hard, but you don't want them mushy.

4. Next, check the broth. Add sweetener, salt, pepper, and a dash or two of Nature's Seasoning to taste. (I put the broth in a coffee cup, taste it, and play with it from there.) This dish should end up with a nice, flavorful broth where you can taste the bacon and a touch of sweetness.

NOTE: You can make this dish a day in advance and let the flavors blend. When reheating to serve, let it cook a little longer to finish it up.

BOBBY'S TOMATO PIE

SERVING SIZE: 6 | **PREP TIME:** 15 MINS | **COOKING TIME:** 45 MINS

𝒯he tomato pie originated in Italy, but history has it here in the South as far back as the 1830s when it included meat, which, as time went on, was excluded. One thing is for sure, if you love tomatoes, you will LOVE this pie, and here in the South, Duke's Mayonnaise is a must!

INGREDIENTS

- 1 9-inch deep-dish pie crust, unbaked
- 5 large tomatoes, peeled, chopped, and drained
- 1 medium Vidalia or sweet onion, chopped fine
- 3 teaspoons dried basil
- 2 teaspoons dried oregano
- 2 to 3 good shakes garlic powder
- Salt and pepper to taste
- Nature's Seasoning to taste
- 1 ¾ cups sharp cheddar cheese, grated and divided
- 1 to 1 ½ cups mayonnaise
- 2 eggs
- Salt and pepper to taste
- Regular or smoked paprika (smoked is my choice)

DIRECTIONS

1. Bake pie crust for 10 minutes at 375 degrees Fahrenheit. Remove from oven, reducing heat to 350.

2. Sprinkle enough cheese to cover bottom of pie crust. Layer tomatoes, sprinkling onions, herbs, spices, and cheese evenly. You want to retain about 1 cup of cheese for the top of the pie.

3. Pour raw, beaten eggs over tomatoes.

4. In a separate bowl, combine mayonnaise and remaining cup of cheese and mix by hand. Spread mixture over eggs and tomatoes (mixture should reach the top of the crust with some thickness).

5. Sprinkle with paprika and bake for 35 minutes.

NOTE: You can get creative with this by adding cooked bacon or even sausage between the layers of tomatoes along with different cheeses. Once you make this, you realize you can add more cheese in the layers depending on your tastes.

BOURBON CARROTS

SERVING SIZE: 4 TO 6 | **PREP TIME:** 10 MINS | **COOKING TIME:** 20 MINS

There are so many ways to cook carrots, but bourbon and brown sugar is a great combination. This dish goes well with ham, beef, or chicken.

INGREDIENTS

- 1 to 2 pounds raw carrots, chopped into small bites
- 1 stick (8 tablespoons) butter, melted
- ⅓ cup brown sugar
- ⅓ cup bourbon of choice
- Salt and pepper

DIRECTIONS

1. Boil cut carrots in water until tender, approximately 20 minutes. (You don't want them mushy.)

2. Drain carrots and return to pot. Add melted butter, bourbon, and brown sugar. Mix well and set on low heat, stirring for a couple of minutes.

3. Add salt and pepper to taste and serve. Again, depending on how many carrots you use, you can adjust the butter and bourbon.

BROWN RICE

| SERVING SIZE: 6 | PREP TIME: 5 MINS | COOKING TIME: 1 HR |

*B*rown Rice is an old Southern recipe. My mother, grandmother, and great-grandmother, Mama, made it. Growing up, we had it all the time, and it was a staple when having friends over. If you look around, there are several variations of it. This one, a family recipe, is delicious and complements almost anything.

INGREDIENTS

- 1 cup uncooked white rice
- 2 10.5-ounce cans condensed beef consommé soup
- 1 stick (8 tablespoons) butter, cut in ¼-inch squares
- Several dashes Worcestershire sauce
- 1 teaspoon dried oregano
- Fresh ground pepper
- 1 6.5-ounce stems and pieces mushrooms, drained (optional)

DIRECTIONS

1. Preheat oven to 400 degrees Fahrenheit.

2. Place rice and soup in a casserole dish and drop the butter squares in. Grind in some pepper, and add a couple dashes of the Worcestershire sauce and dried oregano. Bake for 1 hour, covered.

If you want to change it up, add the can of mushrooms after 45 minutes and sprinkle on top of rice.

NOTE: I usually double the recipe as guests always go back for seconds.

The recipe I am sharing here is a combination of my mother's and my dad's grandmother's. My cousin, Rose Anne Baldwin, sent me the one my great-grandmother, Mama, had written who knows when. She was born in the late 1800s, and the paper she had written it on was old and tattered. Both recipes call for the can of mushrooms, but only Mama's called for the oregano.

White rice, red rice, and brown rice are all-important Southern dishes. South Carolina's first agricultural staple was rice. It dominated the Lowcountry's economy for almost 200 years, influencing almost every aspect of life in the region from the early 18th century to the early 20th century. Rice was responsible for the area's rise to prominence in the Colonial Era. It remained a dominant commodity on the coastal rivers of South Carolina until the end of the Civil War when production started a long decline.

COLLARD GREEN PIE

SERVING SIZE: 6 | **PREP TIME:** 20 MINS | **COOKING TIME:** 15 MINS

*T*his is just yummy, and you can substitute just about any greens for the collards. As usual, I suspect some (cooked) shrimp thrown in might be good.

INGREDIENTS

- 1 9-inch deep-dish pie shell, unbaked
- 1 8-ounce package frozen chopped collards, thawed
- 4 slices bacon
- 1 cup whipping cream
- 1 egg
- 1 cup+ sharp cheddar cheese, grated and divided
- ¼ cup bacon bits
- ½ teaspoon each salt and pepper
- Few good dashes of smoked paprika

NOTE: Interesting fact: Collard greens are South Carolina's state vegetable. Also, cook collards with a ham hock, then pan fry them—they are amazing.

DIRECTIONS

1. Preheat oven to 350 degrees Fahrenheit.

2. Bake pie crust until browned, usually 20 minutes.

3. Boil a pot of water and add collards and bacon. Cook until tender, about 15 minutes. Drain well and discard bacon.

4. In a separate bowl, combine cream and egg. (I always think when eggs are involved, it is best to beat them separately in a bowl first.)

5. Sprinkle enough cheese to cover the bottom of the pie shell.

6. Add drained collards.

7. Sprinkle bacon bits into collards, then add salt and pepper to taste.

8. Pour cream mixture into pie shell and top with remaining cheese. Sprinkle with smoked paprika.

9. Bake for 15 minutes (if all ingredients are warm). This can be made the day before and reheated for 30 minutes or until bubbly.

FRIED OKRA

| **SERVING SIZE:** 6 TO 8 | **PREP TIME:** 10 MINS | **COOKING TIME:** 5 MINS |

*W*hat is Southern cooking without okra? OMG, it's a must-have. No matter how much I fry, there is never any left!

INGREDIENTS

- 1 to 2 pounds fresh okra
- 1 quart buttermilk
- 1 2-pound bag plain yellow cornmeal
- Olive oil
- Smoked paprika
- Sweetener of choice (I use Stevia.)
- Salt and pepper
- Nature's Seasoning

DIRECTIONS

1. Slice your okra lengthwise. Cover in buttermilk and let sit at least 30 minutes.

2. Pour cornmeal about an inch thick into an oblong pan.

3. Remove okra one at a time from buttermilk and lay in the cornmeal until the pan is full. Make sure all okra are lightly coated on all sides by cornmeal.

4. Add enough olive oil to a large frying pan so that when you put the okra in, they will be covered, or almost covered, by the oil. Heat until a small ball of cornmeal and a dash of buttermilk dropped in the oil starts to sizzle. Add the okra one at a time, but don't let pieces touch each other. Sprinkle lightly with paprika, sweetener, salt, and pepper.

5. After 3 minutes, or when cornmeal turns light brown, transfer fried okra to a paper towel-lined plate to drain and cool. Sprinkle with a little more paprika and sweetener. Let one cool and see how you like the taste.

6. If you prefer more sweetener or paprika, add it along with a dash of salt and pepper. Repeat until all your okra has been fried. Sometimes I add a dash of Nature's Seasoning, as well. Let okra cool if you are serving as an appetizer.

NOTE: I serve okra as an appetizer because I can cook it an hour or so before guests arrive and let it sit on a big platter to greet them when they walk in. It is great on its own or with your favorite dip. I like to use Vidalia Onion Dressing that I found at Costco, and you can also order from Amazon. Fried okra can be a side dish for any meat or fish, as well. This is a taster's dish. Cook, adding the seasonings to your own liking, but don't leave out the smoked paprika! Do not skimp when buying okra. It is inexpensive, and people love it. The number of guests you have will determine how much you cook, but I can tell you eight people could easily eat 30 to 40 pieces.

GOOD OLE MAC AND CHEESE

SERVING SIZE: 6 TO 8 | **PREP TIME:** 15 MINS | **COOKING TIME:** 1 HR 10 MINS

INGREDIENTS

- 1 16-ounce box pasta shells
- 2 cups+ milk
- 3 eggs
- ¼ to ½ cup sugar
- Salt and pepper
- 8 ounces cream cheese, softened
- 1 pound sharp cheddar cheese, grated
- 6 to 8 ounces Velveeta cheese, sliced thin
- Nature's Seasoning

NOTE: According to one urban legend, macaroni and cheese was invented by Thomas Jefferson, who, upon failing to receive an Italian pasta making machine, designed his own machine, and had the cook put liberal amounts of cheese in it. The rest, as we say . . . is history. Or is it? Other research finds macaroni and cheese recipes from the late 13th century in southern Italy and, of course, I have always considered it soul food.

DIRECTIONS

1. Preheat oven to 350 degrees Fahrenheit.

2. Boil pasta per box instructions and drain; set aside.

3. In a large bowl, mix cream cheese and cheddar cheese together.

4. Beat eggs in a cup and add to cheese mix along with remaining ingredients, except Velveeta. Stir to combine.

5. In a 9 x 13-inch baking dish, layer ½ of the cooked macaroni, then layer the sliced Velveeta. Add the remaining macaroni, then pour the milk and cheese mixture over the macaroni, making sure macaroni is completely covered with milk mixture. Usually, you can count on adding more milk mixture, and it should be level with the top of the macaroni. Then top with sharp cheddar.

6. Bake for 45 minutes. Once cooked, cut the oven off, and let it sit in the oven about 15 minutes, making sure the middle is solid. This can be made the day before and refrigerated. Just make sure to add milk, if needed, before you cook it.

NOTE: If you really want to make it rich, use 1 cup milk plus 1 cup heavy cream. Also, an added touch would be to add a sleeve of crushed Ritz crackers on top with an 8-ounce stick of melted butter drizzled over it.

HOPPIN' JOHN

| **SERVING SIZE:** 6 TO 8 | **PREP TIME:** 6 HRS | **COOKING TIME:** 45 MINS TO 1 HR |

*H*oppin' John is Southern dish that is a MUST at New Year's Day dinners along with collards and pork. It's a Southern tradition, and every New Year's Day of my life (except for one) I have had it. It makes me laugh when people not from the South don't understand our traditions. I am not coming to your home to eat steak or chicken on New Year's Day. If you are not serving Hoppin' John, collards, and pork, then I am not coming! Ha!

INGREDIENTS

- 1 stick (8 tablespoons) butter
- 1 large Vidalia or sweet onion, diced
- 4 stalks celery, diced
- 1 bell pepper, diced
- 4 to 6 cloves garlic, minced
- 5 or 6 cups chicken broth
- 8 slices bacon, quartered
- White vinegar (optional)
- 1 bay leaf (optional)
- 4 cups black-eyed peas, drained (soaked overnight)
- 2 to 3 tablespoons Old Bay Seasoning
- Cayenne pepper (optional)
- 1 to 2 cups cooked white rice
- Salt and pepper

DIRECTIONS

1. Pull out one of the "Big Guns"—a large pot! Toss a stick of butter in the pot and add your diced onion, celery, and bell pepper, as well as 4 cloves of minced garlic. I am a garlic lover, so I add a couple more. Sauté on medium heat for about 3 minutes, stirring often—you don't want it to burn. The aroma is intoxicating as this simmers. Some people call bell pepper, onion, and celery the "holy grail!"

2. Once the vegetables are tender, add the broth and the raw bacon. You could also add a dash of white vinegar to taste and a bay leaf. Bring that to a boil, and then add the black-eyed peas, Old Bay, and a dash of cayenne pepper.

3. Let simmer about 45 minutes or until peas are soft. Check broth to make sure it has not evaporated. Add liquid as needed. Start spooning in the cooked rice and mix well. You do not want the mixture to be soupy, just very wet. Taste it and decide if you want more of any of the seasonings. This recipe is like a dish of spaghetti or stewed squash—it's going to taste different each time you make it based on how much of what seasonings you add. But it will be delicious each time.

This can be made a day or two in advance, refrigerated, and reheated before serving. Cheat note: If you don't want to soak the black-eyed peas, you can buy two 15.5-ounce cans, drain them, and add them when you add the rice.

NOTE: Most food historians agree that Hoppin' John is an American dish with African, French, and Caribbean roots. The dish goes back at least as far as 1841, when, according to tradition, it was hawked in the streets of Charleston by a disabled man who was known as Hoppin' John. Hoppin' John is also known as Carolina peas and rice. It is served on New Year's Day as it's thought to bring a prosperous year filled with luck.

Collards are also served on New Year's Day to ensure money will be in your future. Pork is served because it is believed to bring good luck as pigs root around with their snouts in a forward motion, and we want to move forward, not backward, in the New Year.

SOUTHERN RED RICE

| **SERVING SIZE:** 6 | **PREP TIME:** 15 MINS | **COOKING TIME:** 1 HR 30 MINS |

*R*ed Rice is one of those Southern dishes that everyone has a recipe for or variation of some sort. Moma cooked it a lot, and we always loved it. My grandmother and my great-grandmother cooked it, and lots of friends cook it. You could count on it at every church supper. The spices can be changed up to suit your taste. It is always going to be good, but practice makes perfect. Most recipes I have seen have the same ingredients, maybe a change up in a couple of the spices or not as much bacon, but they are basically the same. Some people like to put hot sauce or cayenne pepper in it. My friend, Mary Greene, is known for her red rice and crab cakes, and no one can out-cook her on either. I have taken part of hers and my Moma's recipes to come up with this. Mary's was passed down to her. Both recipes are similar. I do not know where Moma got it, or all the other women in the family, for that matter.

INGREDIENTS

- 1 pound bacon
- 1 green bell pepper, chopped
- 1 onion, chopped fine
- 1 6-ounce can tomato paste
- 2 cans water
- 2 to 4 teaspoons sugar (I use Stevia.)
- 2 teaspoons salt
- 2 to 4 teaspoons Old Bay Seasoning
- 2 cups uncooked rice
- 1 pound sausage, chopped into ¼-inch coins (optional)
- 1 pound raw shrimp, peeled and tails removed (optional)

NOTE: It's nice to add shrimp to this to make it a main dish. Just drop the raw shrimp right on top of the rice in the steamer for about 5 to 7 minutes before the rice is done. Make sure the shrimp are pink all the way through. I have tossed my favorite sausage in, as well. I cook the sausage first. This would make a great meal with the Oyster Cream Cheese Curry Ball, Foyer Group Salad, and Lemon Pie.

Charleston Red Rice, or Savannah Red Rice, is a rice dish commonly found along the Southeastern coastal regions of Georgia and South Carolina. The traditional meal was brought over to the United States by African slaves originating from the west coast of Africa.

DIRECTIONS

1. In a large skillet, fry bacon. Transfer to a paper towel-lined plate and let drain. Once cooled, crumble the bacon.

2. Sauté bell pepper and onion in bacon grease for 2 to 3 minutes, then add tomato paste, 2 cans water (use the tomato paste can), sugar, salt, and Old Bay. Mix well.

3. Bring to a boil, then reduce heat, mix well again, and cook on medium-low heat about 10 to 15 minutes and stir a few times.

4. Put the uncooked rice into a rice steamer and pour the tomato mixture on top; stir until mixed well. Steam mixture for about 1 ½ to 2 hours, then check to see if rice is done. Do not stir while steaming.

5. Once done, stir bacon crumbles into the mixture and stir well. I start checking about an hour and 15 minutes into it, as I have had the rice cook quicker.

OKRA PILAU-PURLOO-PERLOO-PILAF

| **SERVING SIZE:** 6 TO 8 | **PREP TIME:** 25 MINS | **COOKING TIME:** 40 TO 45 MINS |

These are all of the individual names for the same okra dish. It is a Southern staple associated with South Carolina, since rice was cultivated there in Colonial days. If you love bacon and rice, you can't go wrong!

INGREDIENTS

- 1 pound bacon
- I large Vidalia onion, chopped
- 1 large green bell pepper, chopped
- Olive oil
- 1 cup chicken broth
- 1 2-pound bag cut frozen okra (cooked according to package directions)
- 2 cups cooked white rice
- Salt and pepper
- Nature's Seasoning
- 1 pound hot bulk sausage (optional)
- 1 pound peeled and cooked shrimp, tails removed (optional)

DIRECTIONS

1. Cook bacon in a large skillet and set aside, saving the bacon grease.

2. Sauté onion and bell pepper in bacon grease until tender. Add some olive oil if it appears you need more to sauté the veggies.

3. Add the chicken broth to the veggie mixture and keep on low heat.

4. Mix the cooked okra and rice together in a large bowl. Pour sautéed veggies mixture in and mix well.

5. Crumble the bacon and sprinkle it in, mixing well. Add seasoning to taste. I like mine with a lot of pepper and paprika on the top.

NOTE: If you really want to go for it, add a stick of melted butter, as well. If you want to make this a main dish, add a pound of cooked hot bulk sausage and/or a pound of cooked and peeled shrimp.

SARA MARSHA RAFTER'S CORN PUDDING

| SERVING SIZE: 6 | PREP TIME: 10 MINS | COOKING TIME: 45 MINS |

$\mathcal{S}$ara Marsha Rafter and her husband, Bill, bought my house at Folly Beach in 2006. We became instant family. She is a fabulous cook and shared this recipe with me. You can spice this up by adding peppers or some sausage. Either way, it's very easy, and everyone goes back for seconds.

INGREDIENTS

- 1 stick (8 tablespoons) butter, melted
- 1 8.5-ounce package Jiffy Corn Muffin Mix
- 1 8-ounce container sour cream
- 1 egg
- 1 15-ounce can whole kernel corn, drained
- 1 15-ounce can creamed corn
- 1 to 2 packets sweetener, such as Stevia

DIRECTIONS

1. Preheat oven to 350 degrees Fahrenheit.

2. Pour melted butter into a 9 x 12-inch casserole dish and swish around.

3. Mix remaining ingredients in a separate bowl, then pour into casserole with melted butter.

4. Bake for 40 to 45 minutes. Don't overcook—pudding will be brown on top when done.

STEWED CABBAGE

SERVING SIZE: 6 TO 8 | **PREP TIME:** 15 MINS | **COOKING TIME:** 30 TO 40 MINS

Cabbage is another great Southern staple. Meggett, South Carolina—which is 25 miles south of Charleston—was the "Cabbage Capital of the World" in the 1920s. My dad grew up in the area and still resides in Meggett on the Toogoodoo River. This is another delicious dish that my family will request, along with my stewed squash, which is made exactly the same way.

INGREDIENTS

- 2 large sweet or Vidalia onions, chopped
- Olive oil
- 1 large head green cabbage, chopped in bite-size pieces
- 32 ounces chicken broth
- Salt and pepper
- Sweetener of choice (I use Stevia)
- ½ to 1 cup bacon bits

DIRECTIONS

1. Chop onions into bite-size pieces and put in a large frying pan. Almost cover the onions in olive oil. Cook on low heat, covered, for about 20 minutes. Check them often and stir so they don't burn.

2. Once they change color to a light gold or off-white and are tender, add cabbage and half the broth. Bring mixture to a boil and stir.

3. Add a dash of salt and a couple shakes of pepper. Put on medium heat and stir every few minutes. Add the rest of the broth as needed if the moisture cooks out. Keep the pan covered and let simmer about 20 minutes. Check for tenderness. Again, I am a taster. Add salt and pepper and sweetener to taste. Use a coffee mug to sample.

4. At this point, add the bacon and stir well. Let simmer 5 minutes.

NOTE: I always make this recipe 24 to 48 hours before serving. (This, again, is a recipe that is going to taste different every time you cook it depending on how much of the spices you add.) I tend to go heavier on the pepper and the sweetener to achieve more of a sweet broth.

SWEET AND SOUR GREEN BEANS

| **SERVING SIZE:** 6 TO 8 | **PREP TIME:** 15 MINS | **COOKING TIME:** 15 MINS |

*R*eally good and easy, and yet another thing that can be made in advance. I found this recipe in Moma's handwriting with her recipes. I have no idea where it came from, but it's a winner—different and delicious.

INGREDIENTS

- 2 14.5-ounce cans French-style green beans
- 1 to 2 medium onions, sliced into thin rings
- 8 strips of bacon, fried
- 6 tablespoons sugar
- 6 tablespoons white vinegar
- ½ cup slivered almonds

DIRECTIONS

1. Drain beans. Pour into a 1 ½-quart dish and cover with onions.

2. Fry bacon, saving drippings. Break bacon into quarters and lay over onions.

3. Add sugar and vinegar to bacon drippings and heat, stirring to combine and dissolve sugar. Pour over onions and beans.

4. Marinate overnight.

5. Heat oven to 350 degrees Fahrenheit. Add almonds and bake for 30 to 45 minutes.

JESSE'S CLASSIC BACON GRAVY

| SERVING SIZE: 4 CUPS | PREP TIME: 15 MINS | COOKING TIME: 15 MINS |

*M*y good friend, Jesse English, shared this secret with me. He is an excellent cook, and you can always count on him for some good Southern food. This is an amazing gravy. It's perfect to make in advance and freeze for later use. If there happens to be a supper party on the radar, this gravy pairs perfectly with any protein—whether it be chicken, beef, or pork. This gravy can be ready to serve over rice, too! Get creative and add any drippings you may collect from your main dish.

INGREDIENTS

- 2 tablespoons butter
- 3 slices thick smoked bacon
- 1 cup self-rising flour
- 2 cups chicken stock
- 3 cups skim milk
- Salt and pepper

DIRECTIONS

1. Using a large skillet, melt butter on medium heat. Cook bacon until almost crispy. Remove bacon to drain, reserving drippings in pan.

2. Mince drained bacon finely, then add back to bacon drippings.

3. Turn skillet up to medium-high heat and slowly add flour and about ¼ of the chicken stock.

4. Whisk flour until browned, then add remaining stock and milk until you have your desired thickness. Add additional milk if gravy becomes too thick.

NOTE: Another twist is to sauté Vidalia or sweet onions in the butter and bacon drippings until very tender to make an onion gravy. Two large onions work well.

Desserts

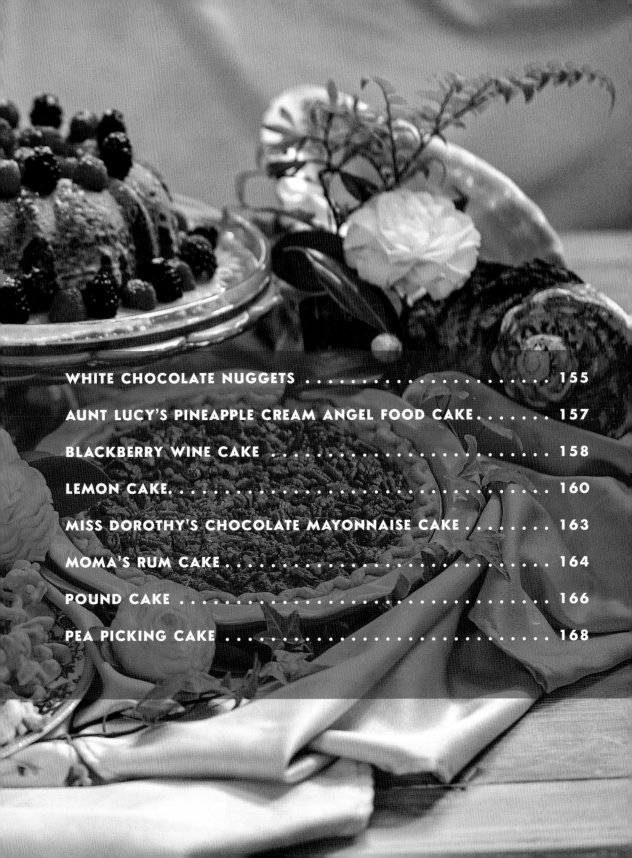

BEST PECAN PIE EVER

| SERVING SIZE: 6 | PREP TIME: 15 MINS | COOKING TIME: 35 TO 45 MINS |

Every Southern cook must be able to serve up a delicious pecan pie! This is a great and easy one—no electric mixer needed. I always double the recipe, freeze one, and serve the other. I have gone through many pecan pie recipes in my life, and this one, without a doubt, is the best. It is not to be confused with a chocolate pecan pie, however. The chocolate chips do not melt, but are an added treat when eating the pie.

INGREDIENTS

- 4 eggs
- 1 cup light brown sugar
- ¾ cup light corn syrup
- ½ teaspoon salt
- ½ stick (4 tablespoons) butter, melted (I use sweet cream.)
- 1 teaspoon vanilla
- 2 cups chopped shelled pecans
- ½ cup semi-sweet chocolate chips
- 1 premade deep-dish pie shell

DIRECTIONS

1. Preheat oven to 400 degrees Fahrenheit.

2. Beat eggs in a large mixing bowl. Add sugar, syrup, salt, melted butter, and vanilla. Mix well. I do this by hand and do not use an electric mixer.

3. Mix pecans and chocolate chips together in a separate dish so they are evenly distributed.

4. Spread nuts and chocolate over the bottom of the pie shell. Pour egg mixture over top.

5. Bake for 10 minutes, then reduce heat to 325 degrees and bake another 25 to 30 min. The key is to make sure the middle of the pie doesn't "jiggle" or move when done.

NOTE: I should give credit to my late friend, Chuck Heath, as I found this recipe in my own handwriting on a notepad bearing the name of a hotel I used to stay at when I traveled for the state of South Carolina. At the top was written "Chuck's Chocolate Pecan Pie." I remember him giving me the recipe, but that's been about 30 years ago now. I guess I just threw it in a box. I found it in the fall of 2019!

LEMON PIE

SERVING SIZE: 6 | **PREP TIME:** 10 MINS | **COOKING TIME:** 45 MINS

*G*rowing up on Sullivan's Island, we would visit the Browne family on Christmas Eve day. They had 10 children, we all went to school together, and our parents were great friends. I remember my parents and the Brownes enjoying lemon pie and Champagne. Sounds like a glorious combination to me!

INGREDIENTS

- 4 eggs
- 2 scant cups of sugar
- 4 tablespoons butter, melted
- Juice of 2 lemons
- 1 9-inch regular pie shell

DIRECTIONS

1. Preheat oven to 300 degrees Fahrenheit.

2. With an electric mixer, beat eggs. Add sugar and beat well. Pour in melted butter and lemon juice; beat to combine.

3. Pour mixture into pie shell and bake for about 45 minutes. (I start checking at about 30 minutes as some ovens cook differently.) It will start to lightly brown on the top when it's done.

NOTE: Guaranteed to be the best lemon pie you have ever eaten! Easy to make and delicious. I make at least two: one to serve and one to freeze. I have also made meringue and added it to the top, though I usually serve it with whipped topping.

CHOCOLATE PIE

SERVING SIZE: 6 | **PREP TIME:** 10 MINS | **COOKING TIME:** 35 TO 45 MINS

I 've heard more than once that this is the best chocolate pie that anyone has ever eaten. So easy to make! Also, if you want to change things up, you can top it with meringue. This pie freezes well, and I always double the recipe —one to serve and one to freeze.

INGREDIENTS

- 1 ½ cups sugar
- 1 stick (8 tablespoons) butter, melted
- 2 eggs
- 3 ½ tablespoons cocoa
- 1 5-ounce can Carnation evaporated milk
- 1 teaspoon vanilla
- 1 9-inch regular pie shell, unbaked

DIRECTIONS

1. Preheat oven to 325 degrees Fahrenheit.

2. In a large bowl, combine first six ingredients using an electric mixer.

3. Place pie shell on a large cookie sheet, then pour mixture into unbaked shell. Bake for 45 minutes.

NOTE: You can tell when this pie is done by jiggling the cookie sheet. If the middle jiggles like Jell-O, it could be ready. If it has a little water-like wave, you need to cook it longer. Also, as it gets done, the top layer may crack a little.

GRANDMOTHER RODDEY'S LEMON ICEBOX PIE

| **SERVING SIZE:** 6 | **PREP TIME:** 20 MINS |

This was created by my maternal grandmother, Marjorie Blankenship Roddey, who was born in the late 1800s. My mother made this pie often when we were children. It was called icebox pie because in those days, they didn't have a refrigerator—they had an icebox. Mama and Grandmama used to make it in ice trays and then cut it into squares. This is a great dessert for hot weather. You can serve it right out of the freezer.

INGREDIENTS

- 6 tablespoons lemon juice
- 2 eggs, whites and yolks separated
- ¼ cup sugar + ½ cup sugar
- 1 12-ounce can Carnation evaporated milk
- 1 Graham cracker pie crust

DIRECTIONS

1. In a medium bowl, mix lemon juice with egg yolks.

2. In a separate medium bowl, beat egg whites until almost stiff. Add ¼ cup sugar and beat until completely stiff.

3. In a third medium bowl, beat chilled milk and add ½ cup sugar. Fold egg yolk mixture into beaten milk, then fold milk and yolk mixture into beaten whites.

4. Pour into pie shell and freeze overnight.

NOTE: The best way to divide eggs is to buy an egg divider. Very inexpensive.

Serve with your favorite toppings, such as Reddi-wip® and berries!

PEACH CHIFFON PIE

SERVING SIZE: 6 | PREP TIME: 15 MINS

*A*nother secret recipe from my friend, Karen Paciulan. Wonderful for a hot summer day! Very light and refreshing.

INGREDIENTS

- ¾ cup sugar
- 1 ½ cups fresh or frozen (thawed) peaches
- 1 envelope unflavored gelatin
- ¼ cup cold water
- ½ cup hot water
- 1 tablespoon lemon juice
- Dash salt
- ½ cup heavy cream, whipped
- Graham cracker pie crust

DIRECTIONS

1. Add sugar to peaches and let stand 30 minutes.

2. Pour gelatin in a small bowl of cold water and stir well, then add hot water to dissolve. Stir well again.

3. Let cool and add peach mixture, lemon juice, and salt. Let chill in refrigerator until partially set.

4. Fold in whipped cream. Pour into graham cracker pie crust and chill thoroughly. Makes one 9-inch pie.

FROZEN MERINGUE

| **SERVING SIZE:** 10 | **PREP TIME:** 15 MINS |

*T*his fabulous concoction was discovered by accident. I made a lemon meringue pie for my nephew, Beckett, for his 6th birthday. I had some meringue left and just decided to freeze it. I had some friends coming for lunch on New Year's Day and needed a quick dessert. So, I ran to the store, grabbed some mango gelato, layered the gelato and frozen meringue in martini glasses, drizzled a bit of Grand Marnier over it all, and voila! Had a fabulous dessert that everyone raved about.

INGREDIENTS

- 1 dozen egg whites
- ½ cup sugar

DIRECTIONS

1. Put your mixing bowl and beaters in the freezer for about 30 minutes prior to making this—it helps mixture get thick quicker. Beat egg whites on high with the electric mixer until peaks start to form. Add sugar slowly, a little at a time, until peaks are firm. Once firm, transfer to a freezer-safe container with a top. Store in the freezer and pull out as you need it.

NOTE: The possibilities are endless when creating desserts with frozen meringue. Think about it: Layer it with ice creams and sherbets and puddings and angel food cake and pound cake! It's a great discovery for a quick, easy, delicious dessert! By the way, Grand Marnier, aka Grand Ma, as we call it in Charleston, is an orange-flavored liqueur originating in Paris, France. It is the shot of Charleston. Yes, we shoot it. No sipping. At one time, Charleston imported it and sold more Grand Marnier than any other city in the United States. It is my shot of choice and a staple in my house.

FRUIT COBBLER

SERVING SIZE: 6 | **PREP TIME:** 10 MINS | **COOKING TIME:** 45 MINS

This is the all-time "Dump Dump Dump" or "Cuppa Cuppa Cuppa." I have even heard it called "Dump Cake" before! It's been around forever, and I am not sure anyone can take credit for it, though they might try. You can play with this recipe and make it what you want by using your favorite fruit—peaches and blueberries are good, and vanilla ice cream is perfect on top! My version is quick and easy, and the batter is so yummy, too.

INGREDIENTS

- 1 stick (8 tablespoons) butter
- 1 cup self-rising flour
- 1 cup sugar
- 1 cup milk
- 2 to 3 cups fruit of choice (fresh or frozen)
- ½ cup chopped pecans or walnuts (optional—mix with fruit)

DIRECTIONS

1. Preheat oven to 350 degrees Fahrenheit.

2. Melt butter in microwave and swish around sides and bottom of an 8 x 11-inch baking dish.

3. Mix flour, sugar, and milk in a separate bowl; set aside.

4. Add fruit to melted butter. I found that 2 cups just did not seem like quite enough for my taste, even though it was delicious. I used frozen peaches, but I think I could have added another cup of blueberries to it, too.

5. Pour batter over fruit.

6. Bake in the oven for about 45 minutes, until golden-brown. Serve warm with your favorite ice cream and maybe a sprinkle of cinnamon.

NOTE: Peach cobbler was invented by early American settlers as a way to use ingredients that were available to them. Peach Cobbler Day, April 13th, was created by the Georgia Peach Council in the 1950s to sell canned peaches.

REAL OLD-FASHIONED
BANANA PUDDING

| **SERVING SIZE:** 8 | **PREP TIME:** 20 MINS | **COOKING TIME:** 5 TO 10 MINS |

*T*his recipe was given to me by my friend, Terry Floyd, about 30 years ago. It was his grandmother Elsie's. I have to tell you, I am a banana pudding snob. I will only settle for the real thing, with custard. I have friends who make a lovely version with instant pudding and cool whip. It's beautiful and everyone loves it, but I have to have the real thing! It takes a little more time, but, oh well, it's so worth it. I cook this every year around Christmastime or for my birthday, which is the 27th. I have been known to eat the whole pan in one sitting. You can't beat it!

INGREDIENTS

- 1 cup sugar
- 2 tablespoons all-purpose flour
- 3 egg yolks
- 1 cup Carnation evaporated milk
- 1 cup half and half
- 1 tablespoon vanilla extract
- ¼ stick (4 tablespoons) butter
- ½ box vanilla wafers
- 5 ripe bananas, sliced like coins

MERINGUE

- 1 tablespoon cream of tartar
- 3 egg whites
- ¼ cup sugar

DIRECTIONS

1. Preheat oven to 400 degrees Fahrenheit.

2. Combine sugar and flour in a medium saucepan.

3. In a separate bowl, combine egg yolks, milk, and half and half. Pour milk mixture into sugar and flour.

4. Stir over low heat and bring to a boil. Boil until mixture is quite thick. Stir in vanilla and butter.

5. Line the bottom and sides of an 8-inch square Pyrex dish with vanilla wafers and sliced bananas. Pour mixture over and set aside.

MERINGUE

1. Beat cream of tartar with egg whites until half stiff.

2. Add sugar and mix until very stiff.

3. Gently spread mixture over custard and bake for 2 to 4 minutes. Watch closely to prevent burning. Remove when tips of meringue are brown. I usually double this recipe for a 9 x 13-inch glass casserole dish.

NOTE: Another variation is to mix crushed pineapple, which has been drained, with the custard instead of the bananas.

WEDDING COOKIES

| **SERVING SIZE:** 24 | **PREP TIME:** 15 MINS | **COOKING TIME:** 15 TO 20 MINS |

*T*hese are also called Pecan Sands, Charleston Sands, Old-Fashioned Pecan Butter Cookies . . . the list goes on. I tried to find some history on them, but no one can really seem to claim them as they are made all over the world in dozens of ways. The one thing I *do* know is they turn up often at events and are delicious!

INGREDIENTS

- 2 sticks (16 tablespoons) butter, softened
- ½ cup white sugar
- 2 cups all-purpose flour
- 3 teaspoons milk
- 1 cup finely chopped pecans
- ½ cup confectioner's sugar
- 1 tablespoon vanilla

DIRECTIONS

1. Cream butter and white sugar; do not overmix. Alternate adding flour, milk, and vanilla, and mix well. Stir in pecans.

2. Chill two hours.

3. Preheat oven to 325 degrees Fahrenheit.

4. Roll dough into small balls about the size of a large marble, but not any larger than a ping pong ball. Put on an ungreased cookie sheet.

5. Bake 15 to 20 minutes until the underside is light golden brown. Check at 10 minutes, as cooking times vary oven to oven.

6. Cool for 30 minutes, and then roll in confectioner's sugar.

NOTE: These are so good. My long-term friend and former college roommate, Kathy Corbett, made these for her daughter's wedding, and I just had to have the recipe because they were MOIST and delicious. I have had what they call "Sands" at events all my life, which these may be. They are always screaming, "Eat me!" They look so delicious with the powdered sugar, but you're always looking for your cocktail as they are always dry. Not these. They are moist and yummy. Best thing is—yes, you guessed it—they can be made in advance and frozen, then thawed out when you need them. I think they could be a great finger dessert at a dinner party and should definitely make it to the sweets section of any cocktail party. My cocktail will still be nearby to enjoy the party, but not to wash down any dry cookies!

WHITE CHOCOLATE NUGGETS

SERVING SIZE: 3 TO 4 DOZEN NUGGETS | **PREP TIME:** 10 MINS

This is fun to make and delicious. I buy the chocolate in thin bars. Very easy to just eat one after the other, and *bang* they are gone! You can play with this one and add other ingredients that you think might be good. M&M's might be fun. Use different types of chocolate. I have used white and hazelnut. This is a great finger dessert to pass around the table after a heavy meal. Wonderful with an after-dinner drink or Baileys Irish Cream.

INGREDIENTS

- ½ pound white chocolate, broken into small pieces, or ½ pound hazelnut chocolate
- ½ cup shelled dry-roasted peanuts
- ½ cup thin pretzel sticks, broken
- ½ cup Golden Grahams cereal
- ½ chopped pecans or walnuts (optional)

DIRECTIONS

1. Melt chocolate in a microwaveable dish.

2. Mix in remaining ingredients and stir well, making sure everything is covered in chocolate.

3. Cover several baking sheets with wax paper, then coat the paper with vegetable oil-based cooking spray. Drop chocolate mixture by the teaspoonful onto the paper and let set.

4. Store in an airtight container. These do not have to be refrigerated.

NOTE: So easy, so good, and best of all, you can make in advance and freeze if you choose.

AUNT LUCY'S PINEAPPLE CREAM ANGEL FOOD CAKE

SERVING SIZE: 14 TO 16 | **PREP TIME:** 20 MINS | **COOKING TIME:** NONE WITH A STORE-BOUGHT CAKE

This recipe came from my great-aunt, Lucy Shealy Hotinger. She served it all the time. It's easy, light, refreshing, and everyone loves it. Nowadays, you can buy a large angel food cake from the bakery in your local grocery store. Talk about quick!

INGREDIENTS

- 1 large store-bought angel food cake, sliced in 3 layers

ICING

- 1 package vanilla (or pineapple) instant pudding
- ¼ cup milk
- 1 20-ounce can crushed pineapple, with juice
- 1 8-ounce container Cool Whip

DIRECTIONS

1. Cut cake horizontally into 2 or 3 even layers. Angel food cake can be frozen and then thawed when needed.

ICING

1. Combine pudding mix and milk, then add remaining ingredients, including juice from the pineapple.

2. Spread icing evenly between cake layers and on top of cake.

3. Keep cake refrigerated until ready to serve.

BLACKBERRY WINE CAKE

| **SERVING SIZE:** 16 | **PREP TIME:** 15 MINS | **COOKING TIME:** 30 TO 40 MINS |

*T*his cake freezes very well. Add the second glaze once you thaw it out. This can be done as many as two days prior to serving. Everyone loves this cake and asks for it all the time. The original recipe came from a coworker named Jamie Saxon. I put my own twist on it with the extra butter, the double glazing, and the fruit. It's a hit over and over again. Makes a beautiful presentation. No one believes it comes from a simple box cake mix. This and my chocolate pie are my most requested desserts.

INGREDIENTS

- ¾ cup pecans, finely chopped
- 1 15.25-ounce box white cake mix
- ½ cup canola oil
- ½ cup blackberry wine (Manischewitz)
- 1 3-ounce box blackberry or berry blue Jell-O
- 4 eggs

GLAZE

- 2 sticks (8 tablespoons each) butter, melted and cooled
- 1 cup blackberry wine
- 4 cups confectioners' sugar, sifted

DIRECTIONS

1. Preheat oven to 350 degrees Fahrenheit.

2. Grease a tube pan and put pecans in the bottom of the pan. In a large bowl, mix all remaining cake ingredients. Pour cake batter into greased tube pan, covering pecans, and bake for 30 to 40 minutes. Check with a long fork after 30 minutes in case your oven cooks fast. If the fork is clean, the cake is ready.

GLAZE

1. While the cake is baking, whisk 1 stick melted butter, cooled, ½ cup blackberry wine, and 2 cups confectioners sugar to make the first batch of glaze.

2. When cake is done, prick with a fork all over and pour glaze over hot cake while still in the pan.

3. Let cool in pan for 1 hour, then remove cake from pan, inverting it onto a cake plate.

4. At that point, make a second batch of glaze exactly as you made the first and pour over cake. Decorate with blueberries, raspberries, and blackberries.

NOTE: This cake needs to be refrigerated. Everything except the second glaze can be made in advance and frozen. To really gild the lily, I pour a splash of wine and/or half a stick of melted butter on the bottom of the cake when it's right out of the oven before the first glaze.

LEMON CAKE

| **SERVING SIZE:** 15 | **PREP TIME:** 10 MINS | **COOKING TIME:** 35 TO 45 MINS |

INGREDIENTS

CAKE

- 1 15.25-ounce box Pillsbury Plus Lemon Cake
- 1 3.5-ounce box Jell-O Instant Lemon Pudding
- 4 eggs
- ¾ cup Wesson oil
- ¾ cup water
- ½ teaspoon lemon extract

GLAZE

- 2 oranges
- 2 lemons
- 2 to 3 cups confectioners' sugar
- 3 sticks (24 tablespoons) butter, divided

DIRECTIONS

1. Preheat oven to 350 degrees Fahrenheit.

2. In a mixing bowl, add all cake ingredients and mix well. Pour into a greased Bundt pan. My preference is Baker's Joy Non-Stick Baking Spray.

3. Bake for about 35 to 45 minutes. You can check the cake with a long two-pronged fork to see if it's cooked all the way through.

4. When the cake is done and while it's still warm, use a long toothpick or skewer (or even a large two-pronged fork) to poke holes deep into the cake. Melt one stick (8 tablespoons) butter and, with cake still in pan, drizzle melted butter all over it.

5. Give the butter a few minutes to settle, then squeeze one orange and one lemon over the cake. Wait about 30 minutes, then remove cake from pan. While cake is cooling, use remaining orange and lemon to make the glaze (see below). Drizzle glaze over top.

GLAZE

1. Squeeze juice from lemon and orange.

2. Mix juice with confectioners' sugar until well-blended.

3. Pour over warm cake.

NOTE: I use a spoon and drizzle in a circular motion around the highest point of the cake so the glaze runs down both sides. The more powdered sugar you have in the glaze, the thicker it becomes. I play with it every time I make it. Sometimes the glaze is thicker than others, but it always tastes delicious. I also like to fill the center with as much glaze as possible so that when the cake is sliced, you can smear some of that yummy glaze on the cake like it's butter! My goal is to never have a dry cake. MOIST needs to be the objective. This entire cake can be made in advance and frozen, and then put the final glaze on it the day before you serve it.

If you really want to go for the gusto, make a light glaze using less sugar (so it is a little watery), and pour that over the warm cake while it's still in the pan. Then, add a thicker glaze after the cake has cooled. It will be super moist.

MISS DOROTHY'S CHOCO-LATE MAYONNAISE CAKE

| **SERVING SIZE:** 10 | **PREP TIME:** 15 MINS | **COOKING TIME:** 30 TO 40 MINS |

Dorothy Keller was the mother of one of my dearest friends, Daisy Guingona. She was a cook, a plant lover, and such a sweet, Southern lady. She was known for this delicious cake.

INGREDIENTS

- 2 cups all-purpose flour
- 4 tablespoons unsweetened cocoa
- Dash salt
- 1 cup sugar
- 1 ½ teaspoons baking soda
- 1 cup Hellmann's mayonnaise
- 1 cup water
- 1 teaspoon vanilla

DIRECTIONS

1. Preheat oven to 350 degrees Fahrenheit.

2. In a large mixing bowl, mix all dry ingredients well.

3. Stir in mayonnaise, water, and vanilla. Mix all very well.

4. Pour batter into a prepared 8 x 8-inch baking dish and bake for 30 to 40 minutes.

NOTE: Get creative! Add Cool Whip or chocolate icing to the top after the cake has cooled.

MOMA'S RUM CAKE

| **SERVING SIZE:** 16 TO 18 | **PREP TIME:** 20 MINS | **COOKING TIME:** 30 TO 45 MINS |

*T*alk about decadent! I made this cake every Christmas for over 20 years for an office I worked in. They loved it and begged for it. It is wet and moist and a bit potent from the rum! You don't have to worry about anyone outdoing you in a rum cake contest. This will always be the winner!

INGREDIENTS

CAKE

- 1 15.25-ounce box Golden Recipe Cake Mix
- 1 3-ounce box instant vanilla pudding
- ½ cup water
- ½ cup vegetable oil
- ½ cup light rum
- 4 eggs
- ½ cup pecans, finely chopped

FIRST GLAZE

- 1 stick (8 tablespoons) butter
- ¼ cup granulated sugar
- ¼ cup rum
- ¼ cup water

SECOND GLAZE

- 1 cup light brown sugar
- ½ cup water
- ½ cup light rum
- ½ stick (4 tablespoons) butter
- 1 tablespoon cornstarch

NOTE: For a chocolate version, substitute 1 box Butter Recipe Fudge Cake Mix and 1 3.5-ounce box instant chocolate pudding. Melt your favorite white chocolate, and drizzle that over the cake instead of the second glaze.

DIRECTIONS

1. Preheat oven to 325 degrees Fahrenheit.

2. In a large bowl, beat all cake ingredients except pecans.

3. Grease a Bundt pan and sprinkle chopped pecans onto surface.

4. Pour batter over nuts and bake for 30 to 45 minutes or longer, give or take, depending on your cake pan and oven. (I always pull the cake out and stick a two-pronged fork in the middle to see if it's cooked through.) Make the first glaze while the cake is baking so it's ready when you pull the cake out.

FIRST GLAZE

1. In a saucepan, bring all ingredients for the first glaze to a boil, then reduce to a simmer and cook 2 minutes. Remove from heat.

2. When the cake is done, pull it from the oven and punch holes in it with tooth-picks. Pour the first glaze over the warm cake.

3. Let cake sit for about an hour before removing it from the pan.

4. Now, if you want to outdo your neighbor, make the second glaze.

SECOND GLAZE

1. Take the cake out of the pan and set it on a cake dish.

2. Melt ½ stick of butter and stir in brown sugar and light rum. Transfer a small amount of the mixture to a measuring cup and stir in the cornstarch until there are no lumps.

3. Add it to the sugar and rum mixture. Bring this to a boil until it has thickened, stirring constantly.

4. Pour second glaze over the cake and down the middle, filling the hole of the Bundt with glaze. Serve with rum raisin ice cream!

POUND CAKE

| **SERVING SIZE:** 12 TO 15 | **PREP TIME:** 15 MINS | **COOKING TIME:** 1 HOUR 30 MINS |

*O*h, my! You have got to have a pound cake in the house at some point in your life. Mine is very dense and heavy. Might be that extra stick of melted butter I drizzled in it! It's a treat when someone makes one for you as a holiday or birthday gift or, of course, as funeral food, though that might be less of a treat and more of a lovely gesture. The original recipe came from my niece, Lindsay Pennell, and then I put my twist on it. It was moist when she made it, and I doubled down on that!

INGREDIENTS

- 4 sticks (32 tablespoons) butter, softened, divided
- 8 ounces cream cheese, softened
- 3 cups sugar
- 6 eggs
- 3 cups cake flour (I like Swans Down brand.)
- 1 tablespoon vanilla
- 1 teaspoon almond extract

DIRECTIONS

1. Preheat oven to 300 degrees Fahrenheit.

2. Cream 3 sticks (24 tablespoons) butter and cream cheese with a mixer. Slowly add sugar. Add eggs one at a time, mixing well after each. Slowly add flour. Add vanilla and almond extracts. Mix well.

3. Grease a 10-inch round Bundt cake pan using Crisco or Baker's Joy and pour in batter.

4. Bake for 90 minutes.

5. When you remove the cake from the oven, give it a few minutes to drop a little, then poke holes in it with toothpicks. Melt remaining stick (¼ pound) of butter and drizzle over warm cake.

6. Let sit about 30 minutes, then remove cake from pan. Sometimes there is an uneven area of batter that cooked around the bottom of the cake—I just trim it off.

NOTE: If you really want to be uptown, cut the cake into two layers and put chocolate cream cheese icing with walnuts on it. Ice between the layers and all over the cake. Other options could include orange cream icing or caramel icing. Or, take 2 to 3 lemons and 2 cups powdered sugar and squeeze the lemons into the powdered sugar until it becomes thick and wet, mixing well. (To make it thicker, add more sugar.) This makes a wonderful glaze, and you can drizzle it all over the cake. Oranges work well for this glaze, too.

The pound cake is a British creation that dates back to the early 1700s. It got its name from the fact that the ordinal recipe contained one pound each of butter, sugar, eggs, and flour. It's not for those on a diet, and you can't eat just one piece.

PEA PICKING CAKE

SERVING SIZE: 12 TO 14 | **PREP TIME:** 20 MINS | **COOKING TIME:** 30 TO 45 MINS

*Y*ummy, delicious, and delectable are the words you will hear when you make this one! This was my Moma's recipe, and she said she got it from her friend, Helen Henderson. Who knows where Helen got it from, because when I posted pictures of it on social media, several people said it looked like what they called "Pig Picking Cake." They had grown up with it at family holidays and such. So, where oh where did it originate? Someone suggested *Southern Living*, but wait—where did *they* get it from? Doesn't matter, just make it.

INGREDIENTS

- 1 15.25-ounce box Duncan Hines Yellow Cake Mix
- 4 eggs
- 1 11-ounce can mandarin oranges, including juice
- ½ cup Crisco oil or vegetable oil
- 1 stick (8 tablespoons) butter, melted (to drizzle over layers)
- ½ cup Grand Marnier (optional to drizzle over cake layers)

TOPPING

- 1 4.6-ounce box instant vanilla pudding mix
- 1 20-ounce can crushed pineapple, including juice
- 1 12-ounce tub Cool Whip

DIRECTIONS

1. Preheat oven to 350 degrees Fahrenheit.

2. Beat eggs in a large mixing bowl. Then add cake mix, mandarin oranges, and Crisco or oil. Mix well.

3. Bake 30 to 40 minutes and check cake with a long two-pronged fork to make sure it is done.

4. When you pull the pans out of the oven, poke with toothpicks, then drizzle melted butter on the top of each while they are warm and still in the pan.

5. Then, if you feel adventurous, wait about 5 minutes and drizzle some Grand Marnier over the cakes. If you have one large cake pan, do the same. My secret to moist cakes is melted butter every time, and if the recipe calls for alcohol, I drizzle that in, too. I don't tolerate a dry cake coming out of my kitchen!

6. Spread topping between all layers and cover cake. Refrigerate overnight before serving. Decorate cake with orange slices or more mandarin oranges. I think you could make some more of the icing and use a fourth cake pan if you are really trying to impress!

TOPPING

1. Pour the pudding mix in the bottom of a large bowl and add the crushed pineapple. Stir well and add in the cool whip until well mixed.

INDEX